SHUT UP,
~~DEVIL~~

SHUT UP, DEVIL

SILENCING THE 10 LIES BEHIND EVERY BATTLE YOU FACE

KYLE WINKLER

Chosen
a division of Baker Publishing Group
Minneapolis, Minnesota

Published by Chosen Books
11400 Hampshire Avenue South
Minneapolis, Minnesota 55438
www.chosenbooks.com

Chosen Books is a division of
Baker Publishing Group, Grand Rapids, Michigan

Printed in the United States of America

Library of Congress Cataloging-in-Publication Data
Names: Winkler, Kyle, 1984– author.
Title: Shut up, devil : silencing the 10 lies behind every battle you face / Kyle Winkler.
Description: Minneapolis, Minnesota : Chosen Books, a division of Baker Publishing Group, [2022]
Identifiers: LCCN 2021049271 | ISBN 9780800762438 (trade paper) | ISBN 9780800762667 (casebound) | ISBN 9781493435883 (ebook)
Subjects: LCSH: Spiritual warfare. | Truthfulness and falsehood—Religious aspects—Christianity.
Classification: LCC BV4509.5 .W527 2022 | DDC 248.4—dc23/eng/20211118
LC record available at https://lccn.loc.gov/2021049271

Cover design by Darren Welch Design

Baker Publishing Group publications use paper produced from sustainable forestry practices and post-consumer waste whenever possible.

22 23 24 25 26 27 28   7 6 5 4 3 2 1

To the struggling, the hurting,
the flawed, the fallen—the human

Contents

Foreword

My gut fisted into a ball. My heart skipped a few beats. And my mind raced ahead to all the what ifs that terrified me. If God allowed me to suffer as much as I already have, does that mean I will have to endure everything that I fear? Though I have walked with God for forty years and have quite a record of His faithful deeds, I suddenly saw Him not as my friend but as someone I could not trust.

How did I get here?

Then I heard the whisper. I sensed the opportunity to return to peace, and I thought to myself, *Oh, Lord, how did I fall for it again?*

Jesus whispered to my heart,

> *My dear Susie, don't you know that the enemy is a horrible counselor? I would never trust him to bring you a message about your future. He is a liar. That's who he is. That's what he does. The devil is baiting you to imagine a future that I'm not in. But no such scenario exists. There will never be a moment of your life that I'm not a part of. I'm with you to the end. And this recent battle? There's no condemnation.*
>
> *But his attack on your soul provides you with information. You let your guard down. You forgot to process*

your pain through the filter of My promises. You forgot all about how My love has carried you this far. You're still standing, my dear girl. The enemy is not winning. You are. You may feel weak, but you are strong in Me. You may feel outmanned, but all of heaven is on your side. You may feel under your circumstances, but you're actually under My wing. Rise up. Declare what's true. And say it like you mean it.

The enemy may be cunning, but he is also predictable. He may operate with evil intent, but at every turn, God has equipped us to overcome. Why then do so many Christians live life beneath their spiritual privilege? Why do so many live without any sense of freedom or victory? Because we need to be trained to stand in battle. We need to know how to shove the enemy off our land when he trespasses. We need to know how to shut him up when he thinks he can speak to us. And we need to know how to enjoy the love of God when chaos swirls all around us.

That is why I am thrilled about Kyle's new book, *Shut Up, Devil*. Using biblical wisdom, neuroscience and his own experience in battle, Kyle will help you silence the enemy's taunts, break free from the lies that bind you and live life with bold, humble faith.

This will be a healing journey for many. As you decide to be honest about the lies you picked up when life let you down, you will find one opportunity after another to walk in new and powerful levels of freedom and wholeness.

Go through this book slowly.

And be changed forever.

Susie Larson, talk radio host,
bestselling author, national speaker

Acknowledgments

This book is far from the work of my hands alone. It is the product of many hands that upheld me from start to finish with encouragement, wisdom and prayers.

To the team at Chosen Books, especially Jane Campbell, David Sluka and Kate Deppe: Thank you for your belief in this project and me. I am grateful for the opportunity to reach people with you!

To my editor, Lori Janke: Thank you for your work with my words; you have made this message better.

To the partners of Kyle Winkler Ministries: I could not have completed this project without your generosity and prayers. Each of you share in the reward of the lives impacted through this book.

To Susie Larson: Your voice of grace has markedly shaped my style and story. I am honored by your contribution to this book, and I am forever grateful for the wisdom you imparted into it.

To my closest friends—Josh, Chandra, Dr. Jim and Leo: Thank you for always picking up the phone and answering my texts. In your own ways, you each helped to flesh out my ideas, motivate me when I was tired and keep me sane through the throes of writing.

Finally, to my family: Your support has done more to shut up the devil in my life than you could ever know. Thank you!

1

The Slanderer

When you imagine a lion, what comes to your mind?

For me, I envision a lion's strong, giant, catlike torso that is covered with a tan coat and moving with a cocky strut. I see his unflinching facial expression, made by a stoic stare and down-turned mouth, all surrounded by a wispy, reddish-brown mane. I wince at the thought of his jaw-stretching yawn that exposes all four of his three-inch canine teeth. I can almost hear his ground-shaking roar.

Thoughts of encountering such a beast in the wild are enough to induce paralyzing fear into most of us. But those familiar with the lion's ways, like his peers in the animal kingdom, know that behind that ferocious exterior is good reason not to be afraid. A lion has a relatively small heart and lungs in relation to the rest of its body. What this means is that it is an incredibly inefficient runner. In fact, the lion is considered one of the slowest runners in the animal kingdom. While it can reach up to fifty miles per hour, it can only do so in short bursts. A lion simply does not have much stamina.[1]

Being a sprinter rather than a marathon runner affects how the lion hunts. When it happens upon one of its favorite meals, such as a wildebeest, zebra or antelope, it cannot launch after it in the moment. Any of those animals would likely outrun it in the long run. So it stalks.

Later in this chapter, I will discuss the particulars of what a lion does when it decides to attack. But perhaps you are wondering why I am detailing the biology and behaviors of a lion. What does a lion have to do with shutting up the devil? Everything.

Stay Alert!

Writing to battle-weary Christians, the apostle Peter warned, "Stay alert! Watch out for your great enemy, the devil. He prowls around like a roaring lion, looking for someone to devour" (1 Peter 5:8).

As with all illustrations in the Bible, Peter's likening of the devil to a lion is not coincidental. It is strategic and insightful. Peter penned this at a time when wild lions still roamed parts of the Middle East. Whereas most of us only know lions from what we see on TV or in captivity, Peter and his original readers were familiar with how they behaved in their natural habitat. To them, a lion was not a rare or even somewhat mythical creature—it was a very real threat of which they needed to be ever mindful. Peter warned his readers that this lion was like the devil.

As I begin a book about shutting up the devil, I understand that I write at a time when the very idea of his existence is debated. Today, the rise of secularism has minimized many of the issues we wrestle with into merely the products of science and psychology, giving little-to-no room for spiritual explanations or solutions.

Do not get me wrong. I am not someone who sees the devil in everything. But I am concerned that the spiritual side of what we fight, from anxiety, fear, depression, insecurity, offense and so on, is not being fully represented. Too many suffer, therefore, with no effective solutions. I believe this is because we are afraid to talk about the enemy, because we either consider him mythical, not worthy of our attention, or fear that mentioning him is not encouraging or positive.

Certainly, we do not want to give the enemy too much credit, nor do we want to sensationalize him in any way that provokes paranoia or fear in people. You will not find either in this book. Like the lion, behind the devil's frightening exterior is someone who is not so frightening. That is what the prophet Isaiah acknowledged when he caught a glimpse of the enemy. He exclaimed, "Everyone there will stare at you and ask, 'Can this be the one who shook the earth and made the kingdoms of the world tremble?'" (Isaiah 14:16). When you see the devil for who he really is, you will say the same. This is precisely why we need to talk about him, at least occasionally. People should not be afraid. People should see him for who he really is: a sneaky, but defeated, foe.

The Roar

Following his warning to stay alert, Peter gives a job description of what the enemy does. It is packed into a single word. A single name, actually. It is *devil*.

Just like when you heard the word *lion* certain images appeared in your mind, so it is when you read the word *devil*.

Chances are you thought of a reddish creature with horns and a pitchfork. Maybe you imagined him orchestrating all the evil in the world from his command center in hell.

But to the original reader, *devil* said something specific about how he works against us. That is because the name devil in the original Greek is *diabolos*, which means "slanderer."[2]

Surely, you have heard that word before. *Slander* means, "the action or crime of making a false spoken statement damaging to a person's reputation."[3]

In other words, to slander someone is to tell a lie not only to someone, but also *about* someone for the purpose of damaging them. Perhaps we see this most in the world of politics, whereby an opponent makes a juicy claim about his rival in order that others might see him or her negatively.

During college and shortly thereafter, I worked on a few high-profile political campaigns. I have seen this play work all too often. The claim does not have to be based on any truth. The simple accusation is enough to give people pause. And that is what the devil counts on for you, too.

I believe this is why Peter compares the enemy to a roaring lion. Wildlife experts contend that most of a lion's roars are mock roars that are meant only to intimidate his victim or assert his power.[4]

Beyond its volume, however, the roar itself has little substance.

It is the same with the enemy's slander. The devil is always shouting about your faults, failures and inadequacies. While his accusations may actually be whispers or nagging thoughts that only you can hear, they can reverberate like roars in your mind until you cower to them.

What you need to know is that the devil's roars, while they can shake you at your core, have absolutely no merit. That is because as a Christian, you are in Christ. The moment you said yes to Jesus, the Bible assures that you became a new person who is defined by His character: "The old life is gone; a new life has begun" (2 Corinthians 5:17). This means that even if an accusation contains some truth about something you did in the past, it has no bearing on who you are today. Because God calls you new!

The title of *in Christ* carries with it an incredibly threatening reputation to the devil. Because people who believe that their past is gone—that they are made new and right with God—have an unshakable confidence and courage to follow God's plan for their lives. They can take whatever risks are necessary to do so.

The devil is not as powerful as he wants you to believe he is. He cannot destroy your reputation—he cannot take it away. He cannot separate you from God's love (see Romans 8:38). But his slander that is made of lies and accusations can make you believe some horrible things that can negatively affect every area of your life.

Have you ever heard any of these statements?

- You are a failure.
- You will never be good enough.
- You are unforgivable.
- You are unlovable.
- You are a horrible person.
- You are not a Christian.

These are only a handful of the devil's slanderous roars. What makes them so dangerous is that you might believe that they are true. As it is said, perception is reality.

Here is how it works: if you believe you are a failure, you will never take risks. If you believe you are unforgivable, you will be shackled by shame and a downcast spirit. If you believe you are unlovable, you will hold yourself back from meaningful relationships. I could go on and on. Belief influences behavior.

I know the power of this because this was my story. For whatever reason, in my early elementary years, I always felt like an outsider. This feeling kept me almost debilitatingly shy and insecure for most of my childhood. Not surprisingly, nobody wanted to be friends with the kid who did not talk. And my pathetic athletic ability also attracted the snickers and name-calling for which kids are known.

Suffice it to say, in my first ten years of life, my reputation became cemented as an outcast and reject—in my mind, at least. And even after I became a Christian, the enemy used all those old identifiers to hold me back from the blessings and call of God on my life.

I will unfold more of my story throughout this book, but essentially, until I discovered what I am teaching you, my everyday life was limited by lies. I do not want that for you. I do not want you to spend one more day held hostage to hopelessness, condemnation, shame or the myriad of other battles you might be facing. That is why I am so passionate about alerting you to the enemy's schemes.

The Prowl

Continuing with Peter's warning, we return to his analogy of the lion. At this point, I should note that Peter does not liken the devil to a lion itself. That is, he does not say the devil is a lion. He says, "He *prowls . . . like* a roaring lion."

In other words, the devil *hunts like* a lion. That says so much about how the enemy goes after us.

As I mentioned earlier, a lion's small heart and lungs relative to its overall body size means that it does not have the stamina to chase its prey for long. This changes the way it hunts. Rather than going in for the attack in the moment, the lion studies and stalks its prey. From its study over time, a lion learns the common behaviors, weaknesses and habits of its victims. Then the lion creates a plan of attack, which includes how and when to pounce.

Typically, a lion does most of its attacking at night under the cover of darkness. Its tan coat provides a natural camouflage that blends its 6-foot, 400-pound body into its surroundings. Coupled with its acute sense of smell and excellent night vision, it is able to be extra deceptive, slowly creeping up to its prey completely unnoticed.

By now, some spiritual comparisons should be obvious. Let's pause to consider them.

We know that the devil is slyly deceptive. People do not fall for his temptations and lies because he is obvious. No, as the Bible reveals, sometimes he disguises himself as an angel of light (see 2 Corinthians 11:14). In this way, he uses crafty arguments, half-truths and seemingly reasonable logic to convince people of falsehoods. In the next chapter, we will explore the sneaky way he pulls this off.

But still, many times the devil remains completely unseen, working his wiles behind the scenes, and waiting for the opportune time to attack. Like the lion, he concocts his plan for how and when to attack based off of what he has studied about your life.

To determine how to attack, the enemy looks no further than our weaknesses. Of course, these include repetitive patterns of sin from the past or present. But our weaknesses do not always have to be sins. Sometimes a weakness may be something we did not chose for ourselves, like a personality quirk or a physical disability. A weakness might be an emotional struggle such as anxiety or depression. Our weaknesses may also include the labels that attached to us when hurtful words were spoken about us by others. Whatever the case, we all have something that weakens us.

Knowing how to attack is one thing, but the right timing is crucial to the success of any assault. From his studies, the enemy knows when you are most vulnerable. Your times of vulnerability could include moments of stress, disappointment, anger, loneliness or exhaustion. The enemy collects all this information while most of us are completely unaware. That is why Peter instructs to stay alert. The devil prowls quietly around each of us camouflaged inside of everyday life and waiting to make his next move.

The Attack

Once a lion selects its target, it attacks in a revealing way as it relates to our battles. Usually coming from an angle that its victim cannot see, the lion uses its powerful back loins to hurl itself toward his target. Taken off guard, its prey has little-to-no time to defend itself before all 400 pounds descend upon it. But surprising to most, a lion does not kill by crushing or ravaging. No, it aims its pounce for the head.

When a lion reaches the head of its target, it does not kill its victim immediately. First, the lion plays with it, albeit in a torturous way. With its strong claws and razor-sharp teeth, the lion bites, picks at and thrashes its victim, sometimes for ten minutes or more. But finally, to end it all and secure its meal, the lion goes for the mouth. Its victim dies by suffocation.[5]

Are the parallels between the behavior of the lion and the devil firing off in your mind yet? The comparison is so rich! Once the devil determines his plan of attack, he launches after your head—not literally, of course. Spiritually, though, the enemy is after what your head represents: your mind.

The Mind

The mind is the control center for the rest of our lives. Made up of our thoughts, it affects how we see and interpret things. It dictates our behaviors. It is the bedrock of our beliefs, and it can determine our future. A popular quote puts it this way: "Watch your thoughts; they become words. Watch your words; they become actions. Watch your actions; they become habits. Watch your habits; they become character. Watch your character; it becomes your destiny."[6]

Similarly, the Bible speaks often about the power of the mind to positively or negatively influence us. That is why it instructs to "carefully guard your thoughts" (Proverbs 4:23 CEV) and links personal transformation to "changing the way you think" (Romans 12:2).

A single notion dropped into the mind has the ability to lift us up, but it also has the ability to tear us down and negatively define us. A bit of pity works through you until you see yourself as pitiful. A seed of fear plants itself like a parasite, slithering its way through you to paralyze you with doubts and what-ifs. Undoubtedly, as Proverbs 4:23 continues, the mind "determines the course of your life." With so much influence, it is no wonder that the devil goes after it first.

21

The Mouth

The enemy's ultimate goal is not to play with your mind. This action is only the means to get to what he is really after, which is your mouth. Here again, I am not speaking literally. I am speaking spiritually. In the Bible, the mouth is much more than what you use to eat. Your mouth symbolizes your words, which represent your beliefs about yourself. Jesus put it this way: "What you say flows from what is in your heart" (Luke 6:45). As we will investigate in the forthcoming chapters, your heart characterizes who you are. It is your identity.

You must understand that the enemy does not attack merely for the fun of it. He is not satisfied with only tormenting you or causing you pain and grief. No, the devil wants to get to the heart of you. He works to have you question everything God says about you so that you do not believe it. If he can do that, you will not pose any threat to him.

Recall that *slanderer* is who he is. The end result of his slander is to get you to agree with it by speaking it yourself. If he can influence you to say, "I am _____" (fill in the blank with any negative definition), then he effectively puts his hand over your mouth.

Again, this is my story. After years of rejection, I came to believe that I was a reject. Coupled with haunting reminders of past sins and present struggles, by my early adult years, I believed that who I had become was wrong. Naturally, when I was called into ministry, I almost did not heed the call. I almost kept my mouth shut. All because years of the enemy's covert work in my mind led me to believe that I could not be used by God.

I am sure you have your own story that led you to this book. In ways that are unique to each of us, the enemy as-

22

saults our minds to get access to our mouths to damage who we believe that we are.

Fear Not

At this point, I hope the exploration of the enemy acting like a lion has not frightened you. I hope that it has awakened you to the realities of what might be behind some of your battles. Peter did not make this analogy to spark fear in us but to alert us to the devil's schemes in our lives. He did that so that we could shut those schemes up—and shut him down!

Remember, behind the ferocious and sinister images that fill our imaginations, the enemy is actually someone who the prophet Isaiah referred to as pretty puny. Sure, his roar might sound loud, but for someone in Christ, his accusations are empty. His attacks might come on sudden and strong, but he does not have the stamina to last forever. You can beat him! You *will* beat him in every lie he launches—in every battle you face! I will show you how.

Before we get there, however, we need to explore more closely the mind, which is the devil's playground. By understanding exactly what he does there, you will be able to form a personal battle plan against him. When you are ready, join me in chapter 2.

Prayer

Father, as I begin this book, gently guide me to be aware of the enemy's work in my life. Expose the lies that I have believed and how they have influenced every part of me. From now on, help me to discern quickly any feeling, thought or word that poses a threat to Your plan for me. In Jesus' name, Amen.

Questions for Personal Reflection

1. What do you hope to get out of this book so that you are satisfied with it when you reach the end?
2. What are some of your consistent battles, either emotionally or behaviorally?
3. How might these issues be rooted in the enemy's work?
4. What lies has the enemy used to speak to you?
5. How have these lies influenced your everyday life?

2

The Secret Strategy against Your Mind

For as long as she could remember, Sarah dreamed of inspiring others through writing. She appreciated the healing she received from the myriad of Christian books that she had devoured through the first few decades of her life, and she wanted to return the favor for others. Never having made a grade less than an A- in all her English and literature classes, Sarah thought she had the technical ability for it. She often received glowing accolades from teachers, friends and family regarding her papers, greeting card salutations and social media posts. Because of this, she felt gifted enough.

Finally, in her midthirties, Sarah decided to take her chances on writing her own book. But every time she opened a new document on her laptop, she would sit and stare at the blinking cursor on the blank page. It was not that her mind was empty. It was that her mind was filled with reasons as to why she could not do it, or even why she should not do it.

Sarah was plagued with reminders of times she had failed. She remembered the personal and moral failings that made her feel unusable by God, but she also thought about disappointments that felt like failures, as small as they might be. One example was pouring her heart out on a pithy post to have only four of her 1,028 social media friends *like* it. Then came the fear that nobody would read what she had written. She could not shake the idea that someone far more popular had already written on this topic. Why would anyone read what a no-name like her had to say?

To add to it all, Sarah felt guilty for taking the time to write. With a husband and two elementary-aged children, she wrestled with thoughts of being a bad mother and wife. *You should be spending more time with the kids*, she heard in her head. *Or at least at a job that would contribute to the bills.* With all these thoughts bouncing through in her mind, Sarah battled feelings of inadequacy, insecurity, fear and depression.

When we think of the devil talking, most of us think of dramatic things that are blatantly immoral or destructive, such as "have that affair" or "end your life." But I share Sarah's story to demonstrate how subtly the enemy works in everyday life. Remember from the last chapter how the devil, like a lion who camouflages itself in its surroundings, hides amid your ordinary routines. He plays in your mind with common sense, reasonable and seemingly wise thoughts and notions. Over time, however, these notions work to convince you of something negative—usually something that is hopeless, worthless, unlovable or unforgivable—all to keep you in a comfort zone, to stop you from pursuing a passion, or to get you to give up on a calling.

This is what I experienced when God called me to step out into my own ministry. Barely a month into my decision to follow God's leading, I awoke to a barrage of accusations that shook my very foundation. First, flashbacks of every sin that I had committed since potty training instilled a fear in me that I was not perfect enough to be used by God. Then, all the hurtful words of rejection that had been spoken about me over the years triggered an insecurity in me that had me questioning whether or not I would be accepted in ministry. Finally, some present battles were brought to the surface, suggesting that God could not use someone who struggled with such things. After days of this, I started to believe what I was hearing: I should quit and do something else.

What made this all so convincing was that everything that I heard was true. As in Sarah's story, the reminders were of events that really did happen. The fears came from words that really were said. And the suggestions, too, were based on something reasonable. None of the accusations were outright lies. But that is precisely what makes the enemy's work so covert and deceptive. The devil tells the truth.

When the Devil Tells You the Truth

We often think of the devil as a liar. And he is. Jesus referred to him as "the father of lies" (John 8:44). But let's not be naïve. The enemy has been honing his skills since the beginning of time. Even back in the Garden of Eden, though fairly new on the job, he was crafty enough to convince the first couple to disobey God. I think it is reasonable to assume he has only gotten sneakier.

You see, it is the enemy's goal to convince you of a lie for a damaging purpose, which I will unfold throughout this chapter. But to craft a lie, he starts with truth. He has to.

It would be too obvious if he came out and said something like, "You're going to fail," with nothing to back it up. So he builds his case for why you are going to fail using real evidence from your past and present.

The apostle Paul gives us insight into the devil's strategy. Writing about how to engage in battle against the enemy's efforts in our minds, Paul instructs, "We destroy arguments and every lofty opinion raised against the knowledge of God, and take every thought captive to obey Christ" (2 Corinthians 10:5 ESV). In the next chapter, we will explore how to effectively use Paul's approach against the enemy, but for now, let's focus on what he says the enemy uses against us: arguments and every lofty opinion. These are the building blocks of his lies.

Arguments

We all know what an argument is. It is a way of presenting evidence to persuade someone's opinion. We do this all the time with our friends and loved ones. It sounds like, "You should do this or believe this way because of _____."

But there is a bit more to Paul's idea of an argument than what we read in our English translations. The Greek word for *arguments* is *logismos*.[1] If you look closely at the word, you may be able to discern what English word we derive from it. If you guessed *logic*, then you are correct.

Logic includes fact-based kinds of statements that might also be called reason, rationality, or common sense. Those are all part of what Paul says the enemy uses against us. These, of course, are far from what we would consider or recognize as lies. That is because they are not lies. The arguments the enemy brings to our minds include evidence of things we did, what was said about us, what actually happened or something we are presently facing. Simply put, the enemy's arguments include the truth. These might sound like

- "You were a druggie."
- "You were addicted to pornography."
- "You got fired from that job."
- "You are quiet."
- "Nobody liked you in school."
- "Your father called you ugly."
- "You are divorced."
- "You are unmarried."
- "You do not have children."
- "Your children do not like you."
- "You did not go to college."
- "You are overweight."
- "You do not have enough money."

Obviously, these are but a tiny fraction of the things we hear about ourselves, but you get the idea. When you hear one of these kinds of arguments, it often captures your attention because it is true. "Yes, I did that/was that/am that/feel that/struggle with that." That is when the devil makes his sleight of hand.

Interpretations

Most of us are so hooked by the litany of evidence against us that we automatically accept as truth what the enemy offers next: *interpretation*. He attempts to explain what those things mean about who we are and what the status of our situation is.

Looking again to 2 Corinthians 10:5, you might be wondering, "Where does it mention interpretation?" After all, the verse says, "We destroy arguments and every *lofty opinion. . . .*" Other Bible versions call these pretensions (NIV), presumptions (BSB) or proud obstacles (NRSV). These are all words that describe an opinion or interpretation of the evidence. This is what prosecutors do in court. They never present evidence for the sake of presenting evidence. No, they always have a purpose, which is to convince a judge and jury of their interpretation of what the evidence means. Usually, guilty. In the case of our spiritual battles, the devil is the prosecutor, and you are the judge.

I will pause there for a moment. Perhaps you are asking, "Isn't God the judge?" Yes, God is the ultimate judge. And as a Christian, He has already judged you in Christ as worthy, accepted and right before Him. The enemy cannot convince God of something He has already decided, regardless of how much evidence he presents.

Additionally, God has given you some incredible promises, such as being ever present with you, loving you unconditionally and providing for your needs. The devil cannot talk God into backing out of these, either. But he can convince *you* that these are not true, which is what his mind games are all about.

Using real evidence from the past or present, the devil works to convince you of something hopeless about you, your future or your situation. Here is what his interpretations of the arguments I mentioned above might sound like:

- "You were a druggie; *therefore*, nobody will ever trust you."

- "You were addicted to pornography; *therefore*, you are too dirty to be used by God."
- "You got fired from that job; *therefore*, you are not good enough for that career."
- "You are quiet; *therefore*, you do not have the right personality to succeed in that role."
- "Nobody liked you in school; *therefore*, nobody will ever accept you."
- "Your father called you ugly; *therefore*, nobody will ever love you."
- "You are divorced; *therefore*, nobody will want you."
- "You are unmarried; *therefore*, there must be something wrong with you."
- "You do not have children; *therefore*, you are not blessed by God."
- "Your children do not like you; *therefore*, you are a bad parent."
- "You did not go to college; *therefore*, you are not smart enough to succeed."
- "You are overweight; *therefore*, you are unattractive."
- "You do not have enough money; *therefore*, you are a nobody."

Do you see how each of these statements includes both a fact and an interpretation about what that fact means about you? Do you see how sneaky this is? By using something that really did happen, was said or is present in your life, the devil quickly moves into the realm of hypothetical doom and gloom, often without you realizing it. Cue the insecurity,

31

fear, guilt, shame, depression and about every other negative emotion you might face.

Sights, Sounds and Feelings

Maybe this all sounds straightforward and easily detectable. I must warn you, however, in everyday life, the enemy's lies are almost always enhanced with sights, sounds and feelings that immeasurably bolster his evidence and cloud your good judgment. It is one thing to hear something in your mind, but it is extra convincing when you actually see it, hear it or feel it.

I think about a time when some friends and I were struck with fear while hiking a trail in north Florida that led into some woods. Only minutes away from the sun setting, there was just enough daylight left to see down the first tenth of a mile before the path disappeared into the darkness. With no map to indicate its length or where it ended, the trail was unknown to us; however, we thought it would be a leisurely adventure. So we stepped into the unknown.

With each passing minute, the sun sank deeper into the horizon until complete darkness permeated the woods. As we trekked well into the trail, a thick canopy of sprawling tree branches added eeriness to our exploration. The mystery was exhilarating. After our eyes adjusted, the dark Florida forest presented a beauty different from the usual sun-soaked beaches.

About a half mile in, we still had no idea where the trail led or how much longer we would be on it. Nor did we know what was creating the sudden rustling in the brush just feet away.

That is when a friend asked, "Did you know that bears have been spotted in neighborhoods around this area?" With that question, I immediately recalled a photo on social media of a bear climbing over someone's fence not far from where we were hiking.

This single mention changed everything instantly. My heart rate probably doubled! From that moment, every snap of a branch and crunching of leaves was interpreted as a vicious animal out to ravage us.

The trail turned out to be rather short, barely a mile. We made it through fine. And not surprisingly, the ominous sounds in the woods did not materialize into any bears. They were likely the echoes of bunny hops and wind. As my story illustrates, though, it does not take much for a situation to escalate into anxiety or all-out panic, especially when coupled with very real sounds and feelings.

As I said earlier, the enemy's tricks are not anything new. He has been using these tactics against God's people since the beginning. They are what nearly convinced Israel to stop their pursuit of the Promised Land. Do you know the story?

When God freed His people from being in slavery to the Egyptians, he freed them with a promise of their own land, a country called Canaan. This land was to be a fertile and prosperous place in which they could enjoy and worship God forever.

Israel's journey out of Egypt toward Canaan took far longer than it should have. But that is another story. What happened on the edge of their promise is the point of this lesson. As they drew close to Canaan, God instructed their leader, Moses, to send twelve men to explore the land (see Numbers 13).

After forty days of exploration, the men returned with some facts. They confirmed how beautiful and bountiful the land was. They also brought back samples of its fruit. Then they revealed something else: "The people living there are powerful, and their towns are large and fortified. We even saw giants there, the descendants of Anak" (Numbers 13:28).

The reality of powerful giants in their Promised Land overshadowed all the positive aspects that they had seen. It also seemed to fog their minds, causing them to forget God's promises. The people shuddered from the *interpretation* of what that reality meant. And at least ten of the twelve men agreed, "We can't go up against them! They are stronger than we are" (verse 31).

This report then spread throughout the rest of the nation, striking fear in the community. The people "began weeping aloud, and they cried all night" (Numbers 14:1). The emotions grew so intense that the people were sure they were going to die.

We will return to this story later in the book. But as you see, a few facts, feelings and one negative interpretation is all that was needed for hopelessness and depression to reign, even in people who had previously witnessed some of the most incredible miracles of God.

Your Ultimate Reality

Did the reality of giants in Israel's Promised Land mean they would face certain doom? Were the sounds in the woods the signs of a bloodthirsty bear about to ravage my friends and me? Did the words of rejection that were spoken about me in my youth mean that people would not accept me in ministry today? Did Sarah's time spent pursuing her dream of writing a book mean that she was a bad mom? No, no, no and no. And what you see, hear or feel today does not mean what you are being told it means, either.

Remember, Paul said that the enemy raises his arguments and opinions "against the knowledge of God" (2 Corinthians 10:5 ESV). This means that he attempts to make his evidence seem more real than the truth of God's Word. This is done to paralyze you, hold you back and keep you quiet. After all, what could incite more insecurity than believing you are someone nobody will accept? What could raise more anxiety than believing God has left you? Or what could provoke more fear than believing nobody will ever love you? This is why I contend that all our battles happen in our minds. In one way or another, they are the result of what we believe.

Hear this: just because you messed up in your past does not mean that you are a mess-up. The fact that somebody in your history did not want you does not mean that you are unlovable by everyone in your future. Being let go of your job does not mean certain bankruptcy. Even bankruptcy does not mean the end of you. Your struggles today do not make you someone God cannot use. In other words, the fact that something is not perfect in your past or present does not mean that you cannot realize your dreams and all that God has for you.

No, God's Word is more real than what you feel! It is your ultimate reality, and the only real interpreter of what your past, present and future mean. You must set your mind on this truth. It is the first step to ending your battles. In the next chapter, I will show you how.

Prayer

Father, help me not to see my circumstances as evidence of hopelessness or doom. Even now as all kinds of thoughts race through my mind, I come to You that I might hear Your Word louder than any lies. Fill me with faith in what You say about me. May Yours be the only voice that defines my reality and determines my destiny. In Jesus' name, Amen.

Questions for Personal Reflection

1. Do you recognize any of the enemy's subtle, convincing whispers in your everyday life? When do you hear them? What do they say?

2. What are some of the "facts" you often hear about yourself and your situations?

3. What are you being told that these "facts" mean?

4. How have feelings made the enemy's lies more convincing?

5. How do these "facts," feelings and interpretations compare with what you know God says about you or your situation?

3

Mastering Your Mind

We all know that the brain is complex. Scientists say that it is not only the body's most complex organ, but also the most complex object in the entire universe.[1] Undoubtedly, by the time you read this, there will be new discoveries about what happens in our heads.

What we know for sure is that the brain was created by God to be moldable. Scientists call this *plasticity*.[2] Now, please do not get intimidated by that word. When you read *plasticity*, think of plastic, which is flexible and transformable. That is how God designed your mind. And while your brain is especially moldable in your youth, you never reach an age where it cannot be changed.[3] At any age, what you see, hear, taste, smell and feel all work to shape your brain. Upon the first experience of something, the brain absorbs it as a memory. When that experience (or something similar) happens repeatedly, that is when the molding happens. This creates a pathway.[4]

A pathway is a route that always leads to the same destination. And it is an intelligent way for the brain to conserve energy. When it detects something that it has encountered before, it automatically takes an action that it has already learned. The thought travels down a pathway.

I am several years into learning how to play the piano. Along the way, I have realized how useful the mind's design is for learning. Often, when I begin a new song, especially one that requires complicated finger movements, I think to myself, *I'm not sure I'll be able to get this one down*. But thankfully, that has not happened yet. The more I practice a song, the more my brain associates my finger movements with the notes and learns the pattern of the song. Over time, the movements become automatic so that I can play a song without reading the notes, sometimes even after months of not playing it. That ability is because of the pathways.

Pathways are not only useful for learning an instrument, but also for learning new languages, skills and routines, and adapting to new environments. It is a brilliant design! The brain's pathways affect not only how you think and move but also change how you see. You have heard of the optic nerve, right? It is the nerve in your body that connects your eye to your brain and carries impulses back and forth. Most people think the eye sends more signals to the brain telling the brain what to see. It is actually the other way around, though. The brain sends more signals to the eye telling the eye what to see.[5]

This means that your brain makes sense of not only things you physically see but also how you perceive things. This is why two people can look at the same situation and come to completely different conclusions as to what they are looking at. It is why the glass appears half-full for some but half-empty for others. Simply put, how you see something is influenced by what has happened in your past, such how you were raised, traditions and traumas.

Imagine this design working in God's unblemished creation right after Adam and Eve were brought to life. I am sure that Adam, as he came across an animal, remembered the opportunity God gave him to name it. Nothing about the beast prompted any fear, nor vice versa. Humans and animals lived in harmony with each other. As the first couple finished their evening meal, they had no worry about when or from where the next meal would come. Day after day, as they saw that God provided for their every need, their brains learned to expect God's provision. There was no reason not to. For at least a little while, Adam and Eve experienced God's goodness, saw everything through His goodness and continued to expect His goodness. That is the way God designed the mind to work.

Obviously, things have changed quite a bit since then. For too many, trauma, abuse, bullying, rejection or simply negative environments have taught us to see everything through a lens of pain, distrust or conspiracy. This has developed an expectation of "whatever can go wrong will," which causes us to react in toxic and damaging ways.

Why?

In a word, the devil. The devil perverted God's design. That is what he does with just about everything that God originally created as good. You must understand that the devil does not have the ability to make anything new. Instead, he uses God's designs and alters them for his own sinister schemes. While God designed the mind to expect His goodness, the devil uses the mind so that you expect badness.

The first words the enemy spoke to Adam and Eve were, "*Did God really say* you must not eat the fruit from any of the trees in the garden?" (Genesis 3:1, emphasis added). With this single doubt planted in their minds, the enemy influenced the first couple to sin, and all of creation spiraled down from there. Think about that. Just a single argument caused the world to fall into pain and negativity. Just a single mind trick introduced fear, guilt and shame into God's previously unblemished world. That is all it took. One single thought interjected into the minds of Adam and Eve created a cycle of negativity. And all it takes is one thought planted into your mind to kick off a cycle of negativity in you, too.

Thankfully, God was not taken off guard that the enemy hijacked His design. No, He was prepared all along. The nature of God's design is that your mind can be changed. This means God programmed into it the ability to undo the effects of the fallen world, to block out the influence of the enemy and to be restored to freedom and peace. The Bible calls it the renewing of your mind, and it is the first and foundational step to ending the influence of the devil in your life.

The Renewing of Your Mind

If you have been in the faith for even a short time, you have undoubtedly heard one of the most familiar verses of Scripture regarding the mind: "Do not conform to the pattern of this world, but be transformed by the renewing of your mind" (Romans 12:2 NIV).

This popular verse is often used by Bible teachers as the solution for every personal problem. And for good reason. As we are establishing in this book, your mind controls your life.

But do you know *how* to renew your mind? When I asked that question to a group of frequent churchgoers at a Bible study, every one of the dozen people stared back at me in wonder. That is when I realized that this is a concept in desperate need of practical explanation. Let's explore its three parts now.

1. *"Do not conform to the pattern of this world"*

Throughout the Bible, the word *world* is used to represent the overall culture and what is happening in a particular moment in history. It includes the culture's customs, traditions, theories and trappings. But *world* is not only limited to what is happening in a community or country. It also includes what is happening or has happened in someone's personal history. To relate this to you, your world is what happens around you and to you.

As we have just explored, the design of your mind means that your environment shapes you. Something that happens to you or is heard by you over and over is especially shaping. Over time, these repeated experiences establish a pattern of thinking or believing. This is known as a mindset.

Unfortunately, because of the devil's work in the world, our minds are born defaulted to negativity. Psychologists call this a negativity bias, and it is the reason why you tend to fear instead of trust, expect the worst instead of the best, and react so strongly and instantly to negative situations or words. The moment you were born, your mind was already set to negativity simply because of the pattern of the fallen world.[6]

Beyond your default state of mind, what happens in your personal life establishes your pattern of thinking. I will return to my life as an example. From as far back as I can remember, I always felt like an outsider, which resulted in my being shy and insecure around my peers. Certainly, I did not choose to be this way, but it was the pattern I was born into. What was particularly shaping to me, however, were the experiences that came with my insecurities: rejection and sometimes cruel words by my peers. As these experiences happened over and over again, my brain learned to expect that certain experiences would lead to certain feelings and outcomes. This became a pattern of thinking that frequently spoke to me: "When you meet someone new, they will reject you. So why even try?"

Think about the negative expectations you battle in your mind. Can you trace their root to an experience that established your pattern of thinking? To experience real change, it is important to identify these roots so that you can stop conforming to the pattern of thinking they have created in you.

2. "Be transformed"

The Bible assures that the moment you said yes to Jesus, you became a new person (see 2 Corinthians 5:17). Some call this being saved. Others call it being born again. Whatever the phrase, in this instant your position before God changed from dirty to clean, wrong to right, rejected to accepted. As a result, you were assured eternity in God's presence, and new qualities were deposited in you that collectively make up your identity in Christ.

Even though you underwent a very real and radical change, most of the change happened spiritually. While you likely experienced a new peace with God and a sensation of being cleansed, your memory was not erased, and your behavior was not altered automatically. Think of it this way: your inside was changed, but your outside was not. This is why many Christians still battle with the voice of their past despite God's promise of all things being made new. This is why for the first decade of my faith I protested, "Why don't I feel new?" so often to God. This is why you need to be transformed. But what does that mean?

The original Greek word for *transformed* is *metamorphoo*, which is the root of a word you will recognize: *metamorphosis.*[7] A metamorphosis is not a slight change. It is a complete change from one kind of thing into a different kind of thing. Think caterpillar to butterfly. From its birth, a caterpillar contains inside itself what it needs to morph into a butterfly. However, it still must go through a process to actually become the butterfly. This is the essence of our transformation, too. While your salvation changed and fully equipped you spiritually, a noticeable physical, mental and emotional change requires something on your part, which is the renewing of your mind.

3. "Renewing of your mind"

You are likely familiar with the word *renew*. We renew subscriptions, driver's licenses and marriage vows. To renew something simply means to resume it back to its default position after an interruption.

When you said yes to Jesus, you were made completely brand-new and given a new starting point, a new default. You were spiritually reborn with the qualities of Jesus. I could take up several pages listing out all the qualities of your new identity in Christ, but here are six of the most foundational:

- A new person (see 2 Corinthians 5:17)
- A child of God (see Galatians 3:26)
- Right with God (see 2 Corinthians 5:21)

- Loved unconditionally (see Romans 8:39)
- Complete and whole (see Colossians 2:9–10)
- God's masterpiece (see Ephesians 2:10)

We will unpack each of these and more in the forthcoming chapters. They are only a handful of the new truths about who you are, which is what the enemy's mind games are aimed at to interrupt you and convince you to believe otherwise.

Think about one of the arguments that spins through your mind. Which one of the above truths does it try to keep you from believing? In my case, I recognize that most of the lies I believed through my early adulthood made me question whether or not I was right with God. I would hear things like, "A person like you can't be used by God," or, "Your struggles make you someone God doesn't love." I heard a bunch of arguments that ultimately made me believe for years that I was someone who was wrong. Not surprisingly, as I went through the process that I am teaching you, I came to recognize this belief was at the root of most of my insecurities, anxiety and destructive behaviors. And it is the belief that the enemy kept reinforcing with his lies long after I was born again.

Before we move on, please hear me clearly. If you are a Christian, then you are truly a new person. That is how God sees you, and that is the basis upon which you will spend eternity with Him. For every spiritual purpose, your old life no longer exists. But old thinking patterns often do. And while those thinking patterns do not mean anything about how God sees you now or where you will spend the rest of eternity, they do interrupt you from enjoying the qualities of your new life, such as joy, peace, patience and self-control (see Galatians 5:22–23).

Shutting up the devil does not mean that you somehow keep him from talking. It means that you identify with the truths of what God says about you more than what circumstances, other voices, past regrets or present struggles try to tell you. It means that you have determined that God's Word is more real than how you feel, what you fear or the ways you fail! With your mind set accordingly, when the enemy inevitably comes to interrupt you, you can interrupt him quickly with truths about your position in Christ. This is renewing your mind, and it keeps you from going back down those old patterns and pathways of thinking and feeling. In time, having your mind renewed brings the qualities of your identity in Christ from the inside out. As the Bible promises, changing your thinking changes your life.

Methods of Mind Renewal

So far, we have covered some in-depth spiritual and scientific principles. Now we are about to get practical. To help you make sense of what you have learned so far and to give you a real-world example, I will briefly return to my story.

After years of the kind of battles and ridicule that I have already divulged, by the time I entered high school, I was certain that nobody would want to be friends with me. I figured I would always be rejected. A mindset of insecurity was so well established in me that it only perpetuated more rejection because it made me awkward.

At sixteen years old, however, something amazing and life-altering happened. As I hesitantly tiptoed with two friends into their youth group gathering one Wednesday night, I discovered a relationship with Jesus that I never knew I could have. With it, I felt a love that permeated my struggles and an acceptance far more real than any rejection I had ever experienced.

In this moment of saying yes to Jesus, a spiritual change happened in me. I was cleansed of my sin and made right before God. But as incredible and real as this was, my fears, insecurities and the patterns of my brain were not automatically changed. Sure, I had a newfound hope that they could be transformed, and I suddenly possessed the will for change, but change in these areas did not happen instantly. No, for this kind of transformation, I had to learn the practical process of renewing my mind.

Recall what we explored earlier in this chapter. The word *renew* means "to resume to a default position." As a Christian, your default position is made new and made right in Christ. So the goal of mind renewal is to get your mind back to that reality. And there are two methods to achieve this, both of which are useful in different situations: the defensive way and the offensive way.

Defensive Mind Renewal

We all have moments when a negative thought enters our mind. This is something we often cannot control. You cannot help when someone says something to you that may be insensitive or when a message unexpectedly pops up on your screen that you did not invite. But you can help to ensure that these unplanned or irrational thoughts do not take root in you or reinforce the enemy's narrative that you are "too much of this" or "not enough of that." When a thought intrudes, your peace and sanity depend upon taking two steps in the moment: determining the source of the thought and doing something with it.

STEP 1: DETERMINING THE SOURCE OF YOUR THOUGHTS

In the third chapter of the Bible, God asked Adam and Eve a question. He asked it right after they had given in to the first temptation, and it reveals a simple way to check the source of your thoughts. After their fall, Genesis recounts that the first couple realized their nakedness for the first time, which gave them great shame. Freshly feeling shame, they hid from God (see Genesis 3:7–8). I think that we can relate to that feeling. I know that I can. It is usually not the mistake itself that causes us to hide, but the belief of what that mistake means about us. This is the definition of shame: the belief that who you are is wrong. And this newfound belief, influenced by the devil, caused Adam and Eve to cower from their Creator.

But God came looking. When He found Adam and Eve in the bushes and inquired why they were hiding, Adam sheepishly replied: "I was afraid because I was naked" (verse 10). Now, take note of what God did next. He asked them a simple but profound question: "Who told you that you were naked?" (verse 11). The first four words of God's question make an effective question that you ought to ask yourself, too, whenever a thought pops into your mind that influences a negative feeling. Ask yourself, "Who told me that?"

"Who told me that I am too messed up to be used by God?"

"Who told me that I will always fail?"

"Who told me that I am not good enough?"

"Who told me that I will always live in pain?"

"Who told me that I am unlovable?"

47

To identify the source, you have to look to God's words that are found in the Bible. My Shut Up, Devil! app was designed to help you with this. It presents God's truths related to about every negative emotion that is experienced by humans. Or if you flip to the back of most printed Bibles, you will find a list of verses categorized by subject. The more you know God's Word, the less time you will have to spend determining whether or not what you hear is from Him.

Check what you have heard against God's Word. Anything that does not match His Word and His character is ultimately rooted in the enemy and needs to be countered and rejected as quickly as possible. That is the second step of this defensive method of mind renewal.

STEP 2: COUNTERING YOUR THOUGHTS

The apostle Paul reveals how to counter and kick out the negative thoughts that intrude our minds: "We capture their rebellious thoughts and teach them to obey Christ" (2 Corinthians 10:5). I do not believe Paul chose flippantly to describe the thoughts that bombard our minds as rebellious thoughts, because rebellious is exactly what they are. These negative thoughts go against God's Word with nothing short of the goal of wreaking havoc in your life. To keep them from doing so, it is crucial that you capture them and teach them the truth.

To put it practically, capturing a rebellious thought is a defensive method of confronting the thought with the truth of Scripture in the moment. A fearful thought about something in the future, for example, should be confronted by thinking on a verse related to fear. Hebrews 13:6 is a great one: "The LORD is my helper, so I will have no fear."

Consider this process as you would an arrest. The negative thought is an intruder, and God's truths are the handcuffs. The instant you think the truth, the lie is arrested. It is put into submission before it can take you down the old pathways of your mind. Truth does not only evict the lie. It also begins to teach your mind the proper way of thinking according to your default position in Christ. And that leads us to the second method of mind renewal.

Offensive Mind Renewal

Even better than always being on the defense is learning how to minimize negative thoughts before they influence you. We do this through a proactive method of mind renewal that I call the offensive method.

The goal of this method is to use truth coupled with the design of your mind to reprogram it for positivity. In doing so, when situations, memories from the past, hurtful words or random negative thoughts occur, they no longer take you down to those old, negative emotions and reactions. Instead, they are sent down new routes that lead to hope, confidence and peace. This is the method of real, lasting transformation. Again, the apostle Paul instructed how to do it: "Fix your thoughts on what is true, and honorable, and right, and pure, and lovely, and admirable. Think about things that are excellent and worthy of praise" (Philippians 4:8).

The concept Paul encourages is not a fleeting thought of something positive. It is an intentional meditation on God's truths and what they mean about you, about God and His character, and about your situation today. In the next chapter, I will give you some specific reflection prompts to think through. But my point for now is that you should think about what you are thinking about.

To understand why this works, let's briefly go back to science. Psychologists observe that thinking on a positive thought for even ten to twenty seconds helps the brain store the thought in its long-term memory.[8] This is reclaiming the design of your mind! As you fix your mind on something good, a pathway gets created. Through this process, your mind is reprogrammed away from its negativity bias and begins to think with a positivity bias according to the way God intended. In other words, your mind gets renewed.

The news that you can reprogram your brain to think and be more positive is exciting, of course, but I caution that the process takes intentionality. No habit is formed overnight. And changing the pattern of your thinking does not happen overnight, either. You have to plan to change.

That is what I had to do. I did not transform from being shy, insecure and easily triggered to who I am today with only hopes and wishes. When God led me through the process I just described, I had to be purposeful about reflecting on His truth morning, noon and night. For a while, I carried notecards with Scripture verses on them that related to my issues. I taped Bible verses to my bathroom mirrors. I listened to Scripture passages that were set to music while I drove or exercised. Then I created the Shut Up, Devil! app with its reminder system to help me better remember to keep these truths on my mind.

Still, while I was purposeful, I was not perfect in this discipline. Many times I did not feel like thinking on truths. I wanted to wallow in pity. And I did. Way too often. Heads up! You will likely experience both moments of great motivation and moments of no motivation. The enemy will whisper to you that it is not working. That is why I encourage you to set reminders for yourself. When you do not feel like directing your mind to think on God's truth, reminders can help you get back on track. They can even help if you get distracted or discouraged.

As often as you can, reflect upon God's truths and what they mean about you. In time, you will realize that those thoughts that once provoked intense emotion do not any longer. You will notice that your funks do not last as long. You will recognize that the voices of your past or present do not limit you as much. Yes, you will begin to experience the true transformation that comes with mastering your mind!

And here is an additional tip to speed up the process and make it more effective: use your mouth to help you. It is part of God's design, too. That is what we will discuss next.

Prayer

Creator, reveal to me the roots of any negative patterns in my thinking. Show me what lies the roots are based upon, and lead me to truths to uproot those lies. Empower me with a supernatural motivation to fix my thoughts on Your Word, and as I do, reprogram my mind with confidence in who You say I am. In Jesus' name, Amen.

Questions for Personal Reflection

1. How does your life reflect the qualities of your identity in Christ? In what way does it not reflect those qualities?

2. What are some negative thought patterns and expectations that you currently battle?

3. Can you trace these thought patterns back to a root experience? How so?

4. How might the defensive and offensive methods of mind renewal be effective in your life today?

5. What are one or two Bible verses you can use to stop negative thought patterns when they arise?

4

The Mind-Mouth Connection

Are you alone, or at least around people who really know you? What I am about to ask you to do might get you some strange looks!

OK. With that disclaimer, let's begin. When I say *go*, start counting backward from ten. In the middle of your counting, say your name out loud. (Now you understand why I cautioned you to do this alone!)

Ready. Set. Go! 10 . . . 9 . . . 8 . . .

Did you do it? Did you recognize that as soon as you spoke your name, you interrupted the counting in your mind? You can try it again if you would like. But there is no possible way to continue to count and speak at the same time. The counting will always stop when you say a word.

Your mouth is the only part of your body that can interrupt your thoughts like that. I have only met a few people that I am not so sure can walk and think. But most of us can!

Certainly, you can move your arm and still think. You can smell and still think. And except when I am eating certain warm, chocolate desserts, I can taste and still think. I am sure you can, too!

All joking aside, when you speak, you interrupt your thinking—even for a moment—either to stop the current thought or to guide a new one. This is God's design, which I call the mind-mouth connection. When you learn how to use the two together effectively, they form a tremendous force for shutting up the enemy's voice in your mind and hindering his ability to influence your life.

As with the last chapter, I hope you are okay with a few science lessons. I think you will find them fascinating. But more importantly, you will find that they affirm what has been in Scripture all along. Let's start there.

Science and the Bible

In the last few decades, science has made great progress in its research of the unique partnership that the mind and mouth have with each other. To find this information, all you have to do is browse some of the top psychology websites. Many of their articles on topics such as how to experience happiness, achieve your goals, change your habits or raise your children focus on the power that words have over the mind. We cannot, however, credit science for this discovery. As I said, what they have uncovered is a principle designed by God that is spoken of throughout Scripture.

The first psalm is a great example of the mind-mouth connection and the impact that it has on a person's life. It begins by describing what God's people should do: "They delight in the law of the LORD, meditating on it day and night" (Psalm 1:2).

Allow me to pause to highlight the keyword *meditate* in this verse. To understand the depth of what God is saying, you have to understand the biblical concept of meditation. In Scripture, meditation is the process of thinking and speaking on a concept over and over.[1] According to this verse, God's people should think about and speak God's Word day and night. As they do, the psalm assures they will be "like trees planted along the riverbank, bearing fruit each season. Their leaves never wither, and they prosper in all they do" (verse 3). In other words, using the mind-mouth connection properly leads to refreshment and renewal.

A little later in the psalms, King David suggests he understood something about the connection. He prayed, "May the words of my mouth and the meditation of my heart be pleasing to you, O LORD, my rock and my redeemer" (Psalm 19:14). In the New Testament, the apostle Paul credits the mind-mouth connection as having a significant part in someone's salvation: "If you openly declare that Jesus is Lord and believe in your heart that God raised him from the dead, you will be saved" (Romans 10:9).

These examples are hardly an exhaustive list of the times the principle is mentioned in Scripture. I will interject a few more throughout this chapter, including from the words of Jesus. But for now, I need to highlight another important word that is used in the last two verses. It is the word *heart*.

The Biblical Heart

The Bible makes a big deal about the heart. As you just saw, the previous two verses reference it. Many translations of Proverbs 4:23 encourage you to "guard your heart." King

David exclaimed in prayer, "With all my heart I will praise you, O Lord my God" (Psalm 86:12). In contemporary Christianity, we often hear preachers lead people to "invite Jesus into your heart."

As with most words like this in Scripture, the biblical heart is not representative of the physical body part. It is not the blood-pumping organ in the middle of our chests. We preachers are not directing people to literally invite Jesus into their atriums! Rather, the biblical heart represents the inner self: mind, will, emotions and conscience.[2]

Accordingly, to praise God with all your heart is to praise God with everything in you. To invite Jesus into your heart is to invite Him into every aspect of what makes you, you. To guard your heart is to protect your thoughts and beliefs, which, as the proverb continues, "determines the course of your life" (Proverbs 4:23).

For years I have said, "You only rise to the level of who you believe you are." This pithy quote is based on the concept that I just explained: what you believe dictates how you behave. We see the results of belief on people's behavior all the time. But Jesus further expounded upon how this works, and it involves the mouth. "A good person produces good things from the treasury of a good heart, and an evil person produces evil things from the treasury of an evil heart. What you say flows from what is in your heart" (Luke 6:45).

Do you understand what Jesus means? In essence, your thoughts and beliefs influence what you say; what you say influences your thoughts and beliefs. This creates a mind-mouth cycle in which it is hard to pinpoint which comes first, beliefs or words. It is a cycle, therefore, that can be tremendously difficult to stop once it is in motion. This cycle eventually steers your life, and too often, it is steered in negative directions.

The Mind-Mouth Cycle

As we explored in the last chapter, the experiences of your past, the words people said about you and what your weaknesses and mistakes try to tell you work in your mind to create a mindset that often affects how you see things. And now we have learned that these also affect what you say. Those words create a domino effect on the rest of your life.

The story I heard of a sixty-some-year-old woman demonstrates how the enemy uses this mind-mouth cycle to torment us for years. As a teenager, her parents disparaged her with words such as, "You're not pretty. Nobody will ever want to marry you." Those cruelties were hard enough to hear once, but unfortunately, she did not just hear them once. She heard them many times, both out of the mouths of her parents and replayed in her own mind. Eventually, she began to speak the words herself, which established them as fact in her heart.

You see, that is what words are most effective at doing. That is why Jesus said it is our words that defile us (see Matthew 15:18). That is why Paul explained, "Faith comes from hearing" (Romans 10:17). It is why many Christian traditions have confessions of faith, whereby they repeat certain affirmations. Words have a power as none other to cement beliefs into us, a phenomenon that psychologists call "stickiness."[3]

In the mind of the woman in our example, words certainly worked to make the belief stick that is she is not attractive. While she did end up getting married, she admitted that the idea those words instilled in her—nobody would want her—worked itself out in her life as sometimes paralyzing insecurity and social anxiety.

So that we do not chalk this all up to psychology, remember what we explored in chapter 1. The devil's name literally means *slanderer*. His goal is to destroy your reputation with lies, and the Bible uncovers that he does this in the same way a lion attacks its victim.

As a lion launches for its victim's head to get to its victim's mouth, so the devil goes after your mind to get to your mouth. He does this to establish a lie in your heart that works to defeat you. While I will be the first to acknowledge that the devil is not responsible for every negative emotion, bad behavior or obstacle in your life, he does at least set up experiences and interject thoughts that kick-start your issues. That is why shutting him up is hinged on reclaiming the mind-mouth cycle. Let's explore how.

The Power of the Connection

What starts in the mind comes out of the mouth and transforms your life. That is the mind-mouth connection. And while God created it for good, the enemy perverts that connection for bad. As I said earlier, though, this does not take God by surprise. He always has a way of transforming bad into good and using the enemy's own tactics against him (see Romans 8:28). Just as the devil works in our mind and mouth to shut us up, so we can flip the script on him and use our mind and mouth to shut him up!

The power of the mind-mouth connection is what I discovered that helped transform me from being an insecure boy who was afraid to talk to a few strangers to being the man today who speaks to thousands of strangers. But its power is not limited to only those who are called to ministry. The mind-mouth connection will work in your life, too, in three very transformative ways.

1. Your words stop negative thoughts.

The counting-backward exercise at the beginning of this chapter demonstrates the first effect of the mind-mouth connection, which is that your words interrupt your thoughts. Words literally have the power to shut up the negative voices that are mouthing off in your mind. In your head, you could be hearing *you're worthless, you're a failure, you're too messed up* or *you're inadequate*, but the moment you open your mouth and start talking, those thoughts stop.

Again, this is God's design, and it is the practical application of the defensive mind renewal principle we learned in the last chapter. It is precisely the way to activate the apostle Paul's instruction to capture "rebellious thoughts and teach them to obey Christ" (2 Corinthians 10:5). The moment you begin to speak, the thoughts are pushed out of your mind—at least until you stop speaking.

The point, of course, is to stop the negative thoughts completely, not simply pause them for a few seconds. That is why it is important not to speak just any words but to do what Paul advised—teach your thoughts to obey Christ. In this case, you want to be like that nagging schoolteacher from your youth who caught you whispering. If you had a teacher like the one I had, he or she not only shut you up, but instructed you what to do instead: "Be quiet and pay attention." The way to do this is to interrupt a negative thought by speaking a positive statement about yourself or your situation that lines up with God's Word.

I find myself having to do this nearly every day. If I am battling a financial worry, it might sound as simple as, "God has always met my needs. He is not going to let me down now." Often that is enough to squelch the thought for the moment. But you should be aware that sometimes the thoughts touch something so deep or relate to such a big part of your life that shutting up the negative voice takes more than a one-liner one time. Sometimes you must really contend against the negativity until either the feeling lifts or you get through the event or situation that is causing the mind games.

This is what I had to do when God called me to write books. I was 29 when I was first approached by a publisher about the opportunity to publish. Even though I had gone through some trials-by-fire that gave me enough content to write, I learned that publishing a book was a new level for which I was not completely prepared.

The beginning of the process was especially triggering. I worked for months to complete everything that the publisher needed to determine whether or not we would proceed. New to the world of publishing, I did not know what to expect. I felt, though, that it was promising to get this far. And I could not help but dream about what it might mean for the future.

After weeks and weeks of waiting, I received a simple email that stated, "We decided not to move forward with the project." That brought me back to reality. But it also brought me back to all the rejection from my past. These few simple words of rejection pressed play on a soundtrack in my mind that repeated statements such as, *You're not good enough*, and *You're a failure*.

Had this happened three years earlier, it would have put me in a funk for at least a few weeks. But this time it only lasted a few days. That is because shortly into my pity party, I realized that I cannot allow disappointment to spiral me into defeat again. I had to regain control of my thinking. That is when I used God's Word to stop the negativity.

As those insecure thoughts attempted to define my identity and future, I spoke truths from God's Word such as, "I am confident that God will be faithful to complete the good work that He began in me" (see Philippians 1:6) and "I trust that God is working all things together for my good" (see Romans 8:28).

Again, I must stress that because this situation scratched open some deep wounds from long ago, I could not instantly silence the negative voices. This process was not a one-and-done thing. No, it took days. But the consistency worked. Not only did it keep those thoughts from plunging me into long-term despair, but it helped to guide my mind into truth. That truth kept me encouraged enough not to give up on the opportunity to write.

2. Your words transform your brain.

Recall from the last chapter how thoughts that enter your mind repeatedly work to create pathways in your brain. Scientists observe that words work to trigger and entrench these pathways even more. In studies using an fMRI machine, when patients are exposed to the most common negative word—no—dozens of stress-related hormones immediately release into the brain, and they cloud the person's decision-making skills.[4]

Angry words are worse. They partially shut down the parts of the brain that are responsible for logic and reason.[5] Perhaps that scientifically explains the apostle Paul's caution to be careful not to sin when you are angry (see Ephesians 4:26). Certainly, negativity clouds judgment in the moment.

But over long periods of time, it warps the brain to think negatively consistently.

Thankfully, negative words are not the only ones that transform the mind. Positive words do, too. In the same study, scientists observed that positive and optimistic words change the parietal lobe of the brain, which affects a person's perception of themselves and those with whom they interact.[6] In other words, speaking something positive not only grows your own confidence and courage, but it also programs your mind to see good in others and in the world around you. An entire shift in perception from doubt to trust, hopeless to hopeful and gloom to joy is possible by using your mind and your mouth!

Still, as I stressed in the last chapter, long-term positive transformation requires intention. A single, fleeting positive thought is not enough to give you more than a goosebump. No, you must do as the apostle Paul encouraged and "fix your thoughts on what is true" (Philippians 4:8). This is a process of meditation that involves four steps of the mind-mouth connection. I call them the "Four Rs of Mind Renewal." With paper or a notes app in hand, I encourage you to set aside a few minutes each day to follow these steps, at least until you have received freedom in whatever area you are working.

STEP 1: READ

This first step is easy. Find a Bible verse related to the feeling, situation or battle you are facing. If you do not know the Bible well enough to go to one immediately, that is okay. Use my Shut Up, Devil! app, a search engine or use the topical index in the back of most printed Bibles to help you find one. Then simply read the verse.

STEP 2: REFLECT

Here is the crucial part of this process and what you should spend the most time on. Reflect upon what the Scripture passage means. Use these reflection prompts to guide you:

1. What does this mean about me?
2. What does this mean about God and His character?
3. What does this mean for my situation today?

Be assured that there are no right or wrong answers to these questions. What you see one day is likely to be different another day, depending on how you feel or what you face.

STEP 3: REPHRASE

Using everything you have seen in the Scripture passage, rephrase it into a personal declaration about you or your situation. Rephrasing a verse such as "Don't be afraid, for I am with you" (Isaiah 41:10) could sound something like, "I am not afraid because I know God is with me, and He will never leave me."

At this point, put the mind-mouth connection to work and speak your declaration aloud. I suggest you practice with the example I just gave. I know it might feel weird at first, but press through the feelings and do it anyway.

STEP 4: REPEAT

Throughout the day or at the end of the day, come back to your reflections and your personal declaration. Take another moment to reflect upon what the verse means and speak your declaration aloud.

Remember, just as it takes weeks to form a new habit, so it will take time and intention with this process to transform your mind enough to see results. But as promised in Scripture and demonstrated through science, you are stopping negative thoughts in their tracks and teaching your mind to think according to truth each time you do this.

3. Your words control your behavior.

A group of preschool-aged children was gathered in a room and given two minutes to play.[7] Once the playtime was up, an adult instructed the children not to touch an enticing train set while he was out of the room. The adult did not leave the room for long, only three minutes, but we all know how difficult it can be to resist something you want desperately when it is right in front of you. (That is why I cannot keep chocolate stocked in my house!) For children who have less willpower than the average adult, those three minutes must have been agonizing.

What the kids did not know was that while the adult was gone, their behaviors were being observed on camera. The result? The children who used self-talk were more likely to avoid touching the train. In short, by using their words, they were able to resist temptation.

This children's study is not the only one that reveals the effect words have on influencing someone's behavior. The mind-mouth connection is often observed in athletes, too. In a group of basketball players, self-talk was observed to improve their play while under pressure.[8] A fleet of cyclists saw that self-talk increased their ability to endure the difficulties of training.[9] There are plenty more studies that confirm the same benefits.

Anyone who is familiar with God's Word should not be surprised by these scientific findings that show how words affect behavior. The apostle James likened words to the bit used in the mouth of a horse that controls the way it goes (see James 3:3). James also said, "For if we could control our tongues, we would be perfect and could also control ourselves in every other way" (James 3:2). Jesus Himself used words to resist the devil's temptation during a moment when He was particularly hungry and exhausted. Do you know the story?

As Jesus was baptized by His cousin, John, in the Jordan River, God's Spirit descended and declared an identity upon Him. The Father said, "This is my dearly loved Son, who brings me great joy" (Matthew 3:17). Immediately after this defining word, Jesus went out into the wilderness where He fasted for forty days. At the end of His time there, undoubtedly famished and tired, the devil came to question what God had just declared. Three times, the enemy began his temptation by undermining Jesus' God-declared identity.

The way Jesus dealt with the devil is a model for us all during temptation. He did not think him away or fight him away. But in each instance, Jesus countered the enemy's argument with, "The Scriptures say . . ." (see Matthew 4:1–11). In other words, Jesus used God's Word to demand, "Shut up, devil!"

This is a crucial principle that you can use to end the enemy's influence in your life. While the scientific studies I mentioned refer to self-talk in a general way, I am not advocating for mere pep talks, although there is nothing wrong with an occasional, "I can do this!" And because of God's design, that kind of thing can work to motivate you for a moment. But those kinds of words do not scare the devil. Only God's Word does that. It is only speaking God's Word that the book of Psalms says brings refreshment and renewal (see Psalm 1:2–3).

It is only speaking God's Word that stops negative thoughts and teaches your mind truth that eventually transforms your entire life.

Putting It into Practice

We have covered a lot in this chapter, but the essence of the information is this: shutting the devil's mouth involves opening yours. With your words, you influence your beliefs. With your beliefs, you influence how you see and what you do. That is why victory in your battles depends on aligning your mind and mouth with God's truths. Knowing who you are and what you have in Christ keeps the enemy silenced.

With this foundation, we are ready to move on to part two of this book. This section will help you put all that you have learned regarding shutting down the enemy's most common and crippling lies into practice. Here is how we will proceed. Each chapter is titled according to the lie most of us frequently hear in our mind. To combat this lie, I will give you truth from God's Word that builds your faith in the reality of who God is and who you are to Him. At the end of every chapter, you will have an opportunity to put the mind-mouth connection you learned to work. I will lead you in a personalized declaration to help cement the truth into you. By the way, I strongly encourage you to read these chapters in order, as each one contains principles that are foundational for those that follow.

Be expectant! As you attack the roots of the lies with truth, I believe the byproducts of them—fear, insecurity, hopelessness, shame and so on—will loosen their grip on you. Freedom is a page turn away. Let's go!

Prayer

Father, thank You for Your Words that declare that I am new, right with You, loved unconditionally, complete and valued. Help me to align my words with Yours. In times of negativity or temptation, quicken my mind and mouth with the truth that resists it. As I reflect upon and declare Your truths proactively, use them to change me to be more like Jesus. In Jesus' name, Amen.

Questions for Personal Reflection

1. How have your thoughts and beliefs influenced your words? How has this affected your life?

2. Think about some of the negative thoughts you have battled lately. What is a personalized statement of truth you can say to stop them when they come again?

3. Consider some of the situations happening in your life right now. What are some ways you see God working for which you can begin to praise Him?

4. What is an attainable strategy to help you to spend a few minutes reflecting upon God's truths? Is there a specific emotion you need to work on? Is there a specific time of day you can reflect?

5. Up until now, how have your words influenced your behavior? How might you change your words to help you resist temptation, take a risk or follow through with something God has asked you to do?

CONFRONTING THE LIES

5

"You are still a horrible sinner."

I wish you could spend a day with me and see some of the messages I receive in my digital inboxes. I am sure your heart would break with mine as you read the stories of deeply broken people who are worried about what something in their life means about them, especially in God's eyes.

To be sure, I am not talking about people who are in love with lifestyles of promiscuity or rebellion and who are looking for God's blessing to continue their destructive behaviors. No, I am talking about bonafide Christians, some of whom have been believers for decades, who use their devices as a digital confessional of sorts to admit things about themselves that they hate. They confess emotional and physical struggles that despite their greatest efforts and devotion to Christ they have never been able to shake.

I think of the middle-aged woman at least a few sizes beyond what society portrays is acceptable who has started

71

diet after diet only to be left worse than when she began. She knows God has the power to break food addiction, and she has seen Him do it for others, but she wonders what it means that in twenty years of faith that He has not done it for her.

I think of the young man who has attractions that will not budge regardless of how much he prays or how many deliverance sessions he attends. For nearly a decade, he has heard the slurs from his youth group peers—and even sometimes from the pulpit—about people like him, so he has kept it bottled up. He only allows himself to wonder to someone on the other side of a screen, *Why isn't God changing me?*

I call these people sincere strugglers. Many of them battle much more than some experience. They wrestle with a constant whisper that puts into question the authenticity of their faith. In their minds, they hear shaming accusations such as *You're not really a Christian, You're still a horrible sinner* or *You are wrong.* Not surprisingly, the insistent doubt about their status before God creates its own set of battles. After years of listening to Christians who have persistent struggles, I have found that the belief that something in their life makes them wrong before God is at the root of most insecurity, anxiety, depression or worse.

Perhaps my heart breaks for these people because I understand their plight. Even though I might not have the exact same story as each person who writes to me, I know what it is like to love the Lord and still grapple with things that seem contrary to the newness that God promises. I know what it is like to feel the breath of the enemy against your ears arguing that this or that in your life means God does not hear your prayers, or that you are too dirty or too messed up to be in His family.

By my midtwenties, almost exactly a decade into my faith, years of contending with the same struggles erupted into a verbal protest to God during prayer.

"You've promised that all things are made new," I pleaded. "But why am I still feeling the same old things? What more do I need to do?"

Have you asked God something similar? Maybe, "Why am I still so anxious?" "Why do I get so angry?" "Why do I still think these thoughts?" Or even, "Why am I still taken by the same, familiar lures?" Is there something in you that fears it has to do with a lack of faith or that you are not a real Christian at all?

I cannot answer every *why* of your experience. We live in a fallen world where many experiences are not the way they are supposed to be. But I can assure you what those experiences do not mean. If you have sincerely said yes to Jesus, your struggles do not mean you are not a real Christian. They do not mean you are still a horrible sinner or are wrong before God. As you are about to discover, the reason I can say this lies at the very heart of the Gospel.

The Great Identity Swap

In part one of this book, we explored how the enemy uses evidence from your life to define you in some hopeless way. He argues, "Because you did this/feel this/fell to this, this is who you are." But that is a lie. As a Christian, God does not define you by your weaknesses, struggles or sins. No, He defines you according to Jesus. Purely and beautifully Jesus.

Here is why that is true. The moment you said yes to Jesus—"Yes, Jesus, I believe You are God's Son; Yes, Jesus,

I believe You resurrected from the dead"—the Bible assures that you became a brand-new person (see Romans 10:9; 2 Corinthians 5:17). This is salvation.

The theological term for what happens in this moment of salvation is *regeneration*. That is a big word that simply means, "the formation of something new."[1]

But the first six letters of the word *regeneration* spell a word that far better describes what happens. It is *re-gene*.

As you know, your genes are the traits passed down from your parents that make up who you are. They determine qualities such as skin color, eye color and hair color, as well as the shape of your features and certain personality characteristics. But you and I did not only receive genes from our immediate biological parents. No, we inherited spiritual genes from our farthest back ancestors, Adam and Eve. Unfortunately, their fall to sin transferred a sin nature into each of us, which is why we are inclined to negativity and failure from the moment we are conceived. By no choice of our own, we are born sinners. Throughout life, we act and react from this identity that is the source of our shame and separation from God.

The Old Testament tells the story of God's people trying to overcome their sin nature to obtain peace and acceptance by God. To do so, they followed rigid requirements and made gruesome sacrifices. Still, their best efforts and behavior could only cover their sin temporarily; they could not change the nature with which they were born.

God was not satisfied with His beloved people remaining in such a condition that kept them apart from Him. So He sent His Son to do something they never could. After thirty-some sinless years in human flesh, Jesus submitted Himself to the cruelest form of execution in history, crucifixion on a cross. Hanging on a tree with all His weight held only by nails pierced through His hands and feet, Jesus endured hours of lashing that marred Him beyond recognition.

As horrible as these events were, we should be careful not to confuse the torture of the cross as something that went wrong. Jesus did not arrive to it by surprise or defeat. No, the cross was God's plan from the beginning to fundamentally transform His people and bring them back to Himself.

The Bible reveals that every thrashing Jesus took to His sinless body was Him taking on the sins of humankind and the punishment that sin deserves (see Romans 3:25). The cross was a moment of sacrifice—not like those that had been performed by God's people that needed to be repeated every year. Through crucifixion, Jesus was the final sacrifice that was placed on the altar of the world to take away our sins once and for all (see Hebrews 10:10).

Hanging in our place on the cross, Jesus killed our identity of sin in order that we could have His identity of righteousness. The apostle Paul boasted of it this way: "For God made Christ, who never sinned, to be the offering for our sin, so that we could be made right with God through Christ" (2 Corinthians 5:21). What happened on the cross was no temporary or subtle change. It does not represent a mere covering of sin. It is a complete undoing of it!

Jesus came to swap our identity with His, to entirely regene us with who He is: truly righteous and holy (see Ephesians 4:24). What is more, this great identity swap is not achieved through some complicated means, but it is simply received by belief (see Romans 10:10). To put it personally, the very moment you said yes to Jesus, you got designer genes that transformed you instantly from old to new, dirty to clean, sinner to saint and wrong to right.

The Guard of Your Heart

When I reflect upon the first decade of my Christianity, I see that much of the tension in my life came from trying to make myself good enough and clean enough for God. I questioned my status before Him on a constant basis. *What more do I need to do?* I later discovered that this question did not come from God but from the enemy. It is the devil who is always insisting that there has to be more to do in order to beat us down and wear us out.

The apostle Paul knew how dangerous it is to live as a believer without the assurance of being right with God. That is why he likened righteousness to a piece of armor. Paul details six protective articles that represent what believers possess in Christ: a belt of truth, a breastplate of righteousness, shoes of peace, a shield of faith, a helmet of salvation and a sword of the Spirit, which is God's Word (see Ephesians 6:10–17). Some years ago, I did an in-depth study of the armor for a course I taught.[2] I do not have the space here to detail each piece, but the breastplate of righteousness is especially revealing.

Paul introduces the armor of God by describing its purpose: "to stand firm against all strategies of the devil" (Ephesians 6:11). He then continues, "Stand therefore, having fastened on the belt of truth, and having put on the breastplate of righteousness" (Ephesians 6:14 ESV). Undoubtedly, Paul is intentional about the order in which he listed these articles. He begins with truth because it is foundational in our battles. That is what we explored in the first part of this book.

But second only to the belt of truth is the breastplate of righteousness. As a visual illustration for my course, I used life-sized replicas of every article in the armor. If you could see them now, you would see that of all the pieces of the uniform the soldier's breastplate was the most identifying. It could not go unnoticed.

You will have to imagine it with me. The breastplate was made of plates of bronze or iron that wrapped around the entire torso and shoulders of the soldier. Scaled with these plates, the breastplate reflected the sun and glistened when the soldier moved. Though the plates made it one of the most beautiful pieces of the armor, do not discount it as something for mere vanity. Weighing at least forty pounds, the soldier could not forget its presence. He could not forget why it was on him, which was to protect his heart.

There is that word *heart* again. Recall from the last chapter that the biblical heart does not represent the physical organ at the center of our chests, but it represents the inner essence of a person. Your heart is the core of who you are, and it affects everything about you.

Consider the instruction of Proverbs 4:23 to "guard your heart" with the revelation of righteousness as body armor. The guard of your heart is confidence in your good standing before God that is made possible only by the finished work of Jesus. This assurance repels the enemy's darts of doubt and any does-God-really kinds of questions that are aimed to get at your core. Ever heard one of these?

"Did God really forgive you of that sin?

"Does God really love you with that issue?"

"Does God really have a plan for your life?"

"Will God really meet your needs?"

Remember that the devil kick-started Adam and Eve's shame by pointing them to a fruit. And to answer these questions for you, he points you to all the rotten fruit of your life as proof of why God should not forgive you, love you, have a plan for you, provide for you and so on. Without confidence in who you are in Christ, every promise of God is argued away with a reason you should not have it or do not deserve it.

I cannot stress enough how dangerous it is to live without the protection of righteousness because without it we are prone to striving. At our core, we are desperate for harmony with God. As people who are made in God's image, we are not fully at peace until we know we are at peace with the One who created us.

Just as children desire instinctively to know that their parents are proud of them, we children of God cannot help but crave God's approval—not necessarily of what we do, but of who we are. We pursue it through performance, which is the only way we have learned to get anything. The problem with human performance, however, is that it is imperfect. The minute we trip up and are confronted with the reality of our humanity, we suddenly fear that our status before God is reset. We start all over trying to win back His heart. Do you recognize this ongoing cycle of shame and exhaustion in your own life?

Please learn the lesson that I did. You will battle every insecurity, fear, discouragement and toxic emotion known to humankind if you continue in the crazy cycle of trying to achieve anything from God. That is because you will be in over your head trying to grab hold of something that is impossible to get on your own. You cannot work your way, accomplish your way or behave your way to right standing with God. Helping one hundred old ladies cross the street in a single day will not do it. Giving all your money to the poor will not, either. While those are moral, ethical and kind things to do, they cannot fundamentally change your core.

The main point that the Old Testament proves, and the entire reason Jesus came, is that works do not work. I pray that you grasp the simplicity of the Gospel that Jesus' work, not yours, makes you right with God (see Romans 10:10). That single acceptance provides your greatest protection against the enemy because it takes away all the reason to try to earn anything from God.

Getting to the Root

The battles in the early years of my Christianity were rooted in the shame I carried from weaknesses, regrets and hurtful words said about me in the past. The feelings from this shame are what I thought all my "doing" could fix. But I was always left frustrated, because as hard as I worked, my greatest spiritual disciplines and achievements only provided temporary relief. I would complete a seven-day, juice-only fast to feel back to the same old me seven days later. I would work to achieve some recognition in the church only to be faced again with why I was no good. Thus, my constant question to God was, "What more do I need to do?"

Understanding the truth of my right identity in Christ freed me from the belief that with enough willpower I could fix myself. Instead, I found something far better than becoming a better version of myself. I finally found peace with myself. That is the real power of the Christian life. Peace with God is peace with yourself and peace with people.

Having said that, what I am about to share with you might sting for a minute. But keep reading, because it is the truth that you need to apply to the root of your battles. It is the reality that will do more than relieve you temporarily. It will heal you permanently if you fully embrace it.

Some things in your past and present you cannot change, no matter how hard you try. Sadly, a woman who was molested in childhood cannot go back in time to stop the stealing of her innocence. A soldier who has post-traumatic stress disorder cannot take away the horrors he saw on the battlefield. A person who has biological issues from birth cannot reenter the womb and change the way her brain and body parts came together.

God has the power to miraculously heal, of course, for which you may certainly pray. Additionally, there are psychological and medical coping mechanisms and means of trigger management that may be helpful. But while these might rid you of symptoms, they do not deal with the root of what really matters. What really matters is the shaming belief about what those symptoms mean about you. As I learned, you cannot work your shame away. That is why lasting healing, freedom and peace are ultimately experienced only by embracing the truth that your wrong identity was replaced by Christ's right identity.

Take this in! The righteousness you have in Christ means that despite wrong feelings, you are a right person. It means that despite wrong memories, you are a right person. It means that despite wrong symptoms, you are a right person. It means that despite a wrong history, you are a right person. In other words, Christ rights you despite you!

Freedom from Sin

The enemy's attacks on an unbeliever are very different from his attacks on a believer. In the lives of people who have not put their trust in the saving work of Christ, the devil's goal is to keep them from doing so. Ultimately, he wants to keep people eternally separated from their Creator. This is what the Bible describes as the power of sin (see Isaiah 59:2; Romans 6:23).

We can probably recognize the devil's work to keep us separated from God from our own lives before salvation. If we do not recognize it in our own past, we surely see his schemes being attempted on some of our loved ones. He works culturally through various worldly philosophies and theories to veil the reality of God so that people equate all things to some meaningless accident of nature. He works personally through abuse, trauma, disaster, disease, sickness and every other fallen thing to skew the character of God so that people will not consider a god who would allow such pain. He also targets people through addictions and other vices to consume their focus or even end their lives before they have an opportunity to hear the Good News.

In the life of a Christian, however, these attacks do not have the same result. That is because, as we explored earlier, "our old sinful selves were crucified with Christ" (Romans 6:6). Yes, for those who believe in Christ, the power of sin is broken. They are free from it (see Romans 6:7–10).

As exciting as this sounds, the idea that the power of sin is broken is where many believers get hung up. Because they still struggle with sin, they begin to question if they were ever really a Christian. They say, "But I still sin, I still struggle and I still feel. I guess the power of sin isn't broken for me. I guess I'm not really a Christian."

This is a lie! The devil can only use sin to make us question our status before God. For all the reasons we covered in this chapter, sin can no longer separate us from Him. That is why Paul boasted, "[Nothing] will ever be able to separate us from the love of God that is revealed in Christ Jesus our Lord" (Romans 8:39). We will delve more into this in the next two chapters.

For now, please understand that the Bible does not assure that a Christian will never sin or struggle. Even the apostle John warned that those who claim to be without sin are only deceiving themselves (see 1 John 1:8). Do not fall for the enemy's sleight of hand to link what you do with who you are. As a Christian, what the Bible assures is that though you inevitably still fall and fail, these failures no longer define you.

The incomprehensible meaning of this is that though you may still sin, you are no longer identified as a sinner. After all, you were re-gened with Christ's identity! Victory in your life hinges on renewing your mind to this truth. This is precisely why the apostle Paul encouraged, "So you also should consider yourselves to be dead to the power of sin and alive to God through Christ Jesus" (Romans 6:11).

Notice, Paul did not urge us to *try* to be dead to sin, as if it is something still to be done. No, he said to *consider*, which means to "think about carefully."[3] In other words, renew your mind to the truth that your missteps, mistakes, flaws, failures and shortcomings do not change your status before God.

With all that said, this does not mean that you should not desire or pursue growth in your life. It does not mean you should settle in the place you are today or that God does not care about whether or not you stop sinning. You should, of course, want to be freed from the entanglements and trappings that hurt you, hurt others or draw your focus away from God. Your heavenly Father intimately cares about what you do because He wants the absolute best for your life.

Unquestionably, sin and struggle are not part of God's best for you. I am sure that this truth is at least part of the reason you picked up this book—you are tired of dealing with the same ole, same ole. Trust me, I get it! But I promise you, nothing physical, emotional or spiritual will change in your life until you start believing correctly.

I once heard the late preacher, Adrian Rogers, say, "The me I see is the me I'll be." That is what I found in my life. All the effort from all the years of trying to change things about me never worked to change me; therefore, I continued to produce rotten fruit from the rotten root of how I saw myself. But when I understood the reality of my new, righteous identity in Christ and saw myself accordingly, the real transformation began to happen from the inside out.

Think of it this way: right believing influences right behaving, which results in right living. Too many of us battle because we have that the other way around.

See Yourself in Him

Remember that your right identity in Christ is what the apostle Paul likened to a soldier's breastplate. As we have seen, this analogy is loaded with insight for our spiritual lives. But there is one additional and crucial revelation from it. Of all the pieces of armor worn or held by the soldier, the breastplate was the only immovable piece. It was fastened to him so securely that nobody could take it off! So it is with your righteousness in Christ. It is not merely a quality about who you are, it becomes who you are and is immovable. Nobody and no battle can take it away from you!

As Paul instructed, "Stand therefore . . . having put on the breastplate of righteousness" (Ephesians 6:14 ESV). See yourself adorned in its beauty and glamor, protected by its weight. Go about your everyday life knowing that as a believer, you reflect the Son. There are no ifs, ands or buts about it! You look like Jesus because you are covered in Him.

Now that you have a proper view of who you are, you should be aware that this is only part of the battle. The enemy is also after your view of who God is. How you see God determines how you make sense of what happens in the world around you. This perspective affects your hope, joy and peace. Undoing the enemy's lie about God's identity is where we are headed in the next chapter.

Speak It!

I am not defined by my past regrets, present struggles, flaws or failures, but I am defined by the identity of Christ. Because of my belief and trust in Jesus, I am new and right in God's sight!

Questions for Personal Reflection

1. What struggles or feelings have been used to make you question the authenticity of your Christianity or your status before God?
2. Why do you think these experiences caused you shame while other experiences did not have the same impact?
3. What are some ways that you have tried to work or achieve your way back into right standing with God?

What has been the result physically, emotionally or spiritually?

4. Reflect on the concept that righteousness is received by acceptance and not from performance. What changes will you make in your life based upon that truth?

5. There may be times when you do not feel righteous. What Scripture passages or truths can you tell yourself when this comes up in your life?

6

"God is punishing you."

"Can I ask you something, Kyle?" David timidly questioned as I greeted people in the lobby after a Sunday morning service.

"Definitely. What's going on?" I responded. After a deep breath, David began to share something that had haunted him for nearly twenty years.

"When I was only fifteen, my mom suddenly passed away from cancer," he confessed through tearful eyes. "None of us expected it. One moment she was filled with all the joy of life, and the next she was doubled over in pain and on her way to the hospital. Three months later, she was gone."

As my heart was breaking for the loss of his mother at such a pivotal age, David shared more of his story to me.

"I also lost my father that day," he said.

A bit taken back, I clarified, "You mean, both your mother and your father died on the same day?"

"No, no," he explained. "When my mom breathed her final breath, my dad was almost instantly plunged into despair. For years, he was left hardly able to care for himself, much less my younger siblings and me."

David went on to disclose that shortly after his mother's death, a generous and compassionate couple in his church community saw the downward spiral of his family, and they brought him into their own. While their care met his physical needs, his next question revealed the root of a spiritual torment he had suffered from until the day we talked.

"Was my mom's death my fault?" he blurted out as if the question had been pent up inside him for years.

Before I launched into my answer, I needed to better understand why he feared he was the cause of his mother's death and his family's subsequent grief.

"Why do you feel that way?"

He proceeded to confide that in the season of his mother's sickness, he battled a rebellious spirit. Though he knew God and he loved Jesus, he had questions that he did not always pose in the most respectful ways to his Sunday-school teachers.

"Furthermore," David admitted, "my hormones were raging, and I'm not proud of the things I did in that area of my life."

Rebellion and lust are hardly atypical of a fifteen-year-old boy, but when you are a teenager looking for reasons as to why your world has been turned upside down, the first place you look is inward. Many ask, "What have I done?" For David, however, it was not only his own internal voice making those accusations. He caught wind that church folks were blaming his mom's lack of healing on his lack of faith. Eventually, some even told him that his family's peril was the result of God's punishment because of his sins.

"Was it?" David begged to know. "Were all these bad things that happened to my family the products of God's punishment?" He asked me this as a question, but I could tell by what he later divulged that it was more of a foregone conclusion to him.

Over the years, David had accepted the belief that his sins had brought God's wrath. And though he continued to attend church out of habit, he battled insecurity with God and an on-and-off relationship with Him. But something I had said in the message that morning had prompted him to look up from the game he had been playing on his phone and wonder, "Have I been believing a lie?"

Is God Really Good?

Teenagers are not the only ones who believe that something unfortunate was brought upon them because they upset God. I receive emails frequently from adults of every age who fear that some sudden financial or health crisis is the consequence of God's anger at their failures.

An angry God who is looking for ways to afflict us does not represent Him, but it is the story that the devil has concocted to erode our relationship with Him. If he can do that, he can steal our only source of real power, joy, peace and meaning. The Bible is certain about the character of God: He is good. From beginning to end, Scripture boasts of it. The books of the Old Testament repeatedly praise: "Give thanks to the LORD, for he is good" (Psalm 107:1; 118:1; 136:1; 1 Chronicles 16:34). In the New Testament, Jesus affirmed it (see Mark 10:18). The apostle John did, too, adding, "there is no darkness in him" (1 John 1:5).

Good is the fundamental aspect of who God is. It is the quality from which everything else about Him flows. God loves, heals and provides because He is good. Furthermore, as the apostle Paul revealed, His goodness is what draws us to Him (see Romans 2:4). This is reflected in our human relationships, whereby we naturally draw close to those who treat us well and take interest in our lives. That is not a selfish thing; it is something hardwired into us by our Creator to serve as a means of protection. Nobody wants to be near someone who abuses or misuses them. In the same way, nobody wants to be in relationship with a god they perceive only causes them pain and suffering, takes no interest in their lives or is waiting to punish them. And the devil knows it.

"Is God really good?" is the question the devil has been prompting people to ask from the very beginning. When he probed Adam and Eve with, "Did God really say you must not eat the fruit from any of the trees in the garden?" (Genesis 3:1), what he was really asking is, "Can you trust that God has your best interest at heart? Is He holding something back from you?" In other words, "Is God really good?"

Any talk of suffering brings to mind the story of Job. We have the benefit of knowing what was happening behind the scenes. At the time, however, Job did not know that the sudden loss of his health, children, belongings and dignity were the schemes of the enemy. Rather, he was led to believe that God had done these things. Satan then baited him to curse God's character (see Job 2:9).

Nothing has changed in thousands of years of human history. Still today, the devil uses misfortunes on both unbelievers and believers to take himself out of the limelight and make God look like the author of all the problems. From pain or suffering, such as sickness, he intends for you to ask, "Why did God give this to me?" From trials or disaster, like the tragic loss of a home, job or loved one, he stirs the question, "Why did God do this to me?" Pointing to a personal weakness, struggle or disability, the enemy wants you to protest, "God, why did You create me this way?"

Unfortunately, the concept of an angry God is so engrained into most of us that we never stop to think, *Perhaps what I experienced never originated from God in the first place. Maybe what I am going through isn't God's will, God's hand or God's plan at all.* Instead, we respond as David did to his mom's death, and we look inside ourselves for a reason that we are being punished by God. But are we?

Does God Still Punish?

I regularly hear from people who grew up in religious traditions that they see God as an angry dictator who is ready to punish their every misstep. In my case, I remember teachers at my church's school frequently warning my peers and me to behave, otherwise, "God will get you back!" It is not hard to understand why this threat did not do anything to enhance my relationship with God. It also did not work to keep me from misbehaving.

I do not place any fault on the people who tried to motivate me with fear of God's punishment. I do not think they tried intentionally to misrepresent God's character or cause any kind of distance between God and me. Many only repeated beliefs that had been passed down from others who innocently confused how God relates to people today with how God related to people in the Old Testament.

91

I see this confusion in most who write me today in fear that their suffering is God's punishment. They see instances in Scripture where God destroyed entire cities, sent disease or withheld blessings because of disobedience and sin. Consequently, they assume, "God must be doing the same to me."

Unquestionably, stories of God's wrath against sin exist in Scripture. In the Old Testament, God so hated the chasm that sin placed between Him and His people that at times His anger burned fiercely against it. Still, amid some of God's sharpest criticisms, He gave clues that He did not desire His rage to last forever. While chastising His people for their idol worship, God gave a word through His prophet Isaiah of a glimpse into future grace: "For I will not fight against you forever; I will not always be angry" (Isaiah 57:16).

Why did God give such notice to His people? Was it because He had a change of mind regarding the seriousness of sin? Did He suddenly decide that disobedience was not so bad after all? Hardly. It is because God knew He was about to deal with sin in a way that would satisfy His anger forever.

About seven hundred years after God revealed His intentions through Isaiah, He sent His Son Jesus into this world. With foresight into what Jesus would accomplish, hosts of angels erupted in celebration at His birth. They rejoiced, "Glory to God in the highest, and on earth peace, good will toward men" (Luke 2:14 KJV).

You have likely heard these words before, if nowhere else but on a Christmas card. At first glance, the angels appear to cheer Jesus' birth as the end to pain and trouble on earth. But Jesus Himself refuted that idea: "Here on earth you will have many trials and sorrows" (John 16:33). More than two thousand years later, we still know the realities of these trials.

If not the end of suffering, what kind of peace did the angels announce at the birth of Jesus? The peace of all peace! They announced the arrival of the One who would bring permanent peace between God and humankind. They heralded the One who was destined once and for all to take the anger and punishment God had stored up against sin.

That is precisely what Jesus did on the cross. As we discussed in the last chapter, He hung in our place becoming our sin. Through His crucifixion, "God was in Christ, reconciling the world to himself, no longer counting people's sins against them" (2 Corinthians 5:19). Read that again. What Jesus accomplished does not get any clearer than that! On the cross, Jesus took all God's punishment for sin, thereby ending God's anger and forever establishing our peace with God as the angels had announced at His birth.

Sometimes I fear that we minimize Jesus' work as merely a softening of the Old Testament system. In truth, He fundamentally changed the system, ushering in a new relationship of peace between God and people. Today, because of Jesus' finished work, God no longer sends natural disasters or sickness, nor does He withhold blessings as a threat for us to shape up or as a punishment for how we have messed up. Rather, He uses His Holy Spirit to motivate.

To unbelievers, God's Holy Spirit works outside of them to show them their need for Jesus (see John 16:7–9). To believers, God's Holy Spirit works in them to lead and guide. And while the Holy Spirit's direction can sometimes be strong and challenging, it is never punishing or condemning. What all this means is that God is not mad at you. He is not even in a bad mood! If you have accepted Jesus, then you are at peace with God.

True as this is, however, our world and our personal lives are not always peaceful. Tragedy, trouble and trials abound. But if they are not from the hand of God, from where do they come?

Why Bad Things Happen

Imagine passing by a junkyard stacked with shattered, busted and wrecked vehicles. None of us would look at any of those totaled cars and wonder why their manufacturer created them in that condition, nor would we wonder why the manufacturer did that to the vehicle. That is because we know car manufacturers create vehicles in as perfect condition as possible. They do not create a wrecked vehicle, neither do they wreck the vehicle themselves. No, something else happened that was outside the original will of the manufacturer.

This analogy helps us understand the state of our world and personal lives. Our good and perfect God could not create anything that is not good and perfect. The Bible affirms this. After He completed His six days of creation, God looked upon His work and "saw that it was very good" (Genesis 1:31). Accordingly, you can be sure that the pain, struggle and brokenness you see and experience in the world are not because God wants it that way. There must be another reason for this wrecked world and all the hurt in it—and there is. Three reasons, in fact, that do not have anything to do with God.

Reason 1: The Consequences of the Fallen World

The original sin of Adam and Eve had a catastrophic effect upon God's perfectly created world. This is known as the Fall. The apostle Paul described what happened: "When

Adam sinned, sin entered the world. Adam's sin brought death, so death spread to everyone" (Romans 5:12).

A quick comparison of Genesis 1–2 to the next few chapters is enough to show the radical difference between creation before the Fall versus creation after it. Before the Fall, there was no death nor anything that led to death, such as sickness, disaster or lack. Immediately after the Fall, people experienced shame, pain, wicked and evil intentions, and, of course, death. Even the environment changed. The ground became hard to work (see Genesis 3:17) and vegetation was no longer nutritious enough to sustain human health. That is why God eventually gave the okay to eat meat (see Genesis 9:3).

As Paul said, the first couple's sin did not only affect one or two generations, but it infected every aspect of creation and humanity in ways that snowball as time goes on. Consider sin's consequence on health. Because our food sources do not have the nutrients they once did, our bodies no longer operate as they were designed to. Without the proper nutrients, we do not think as clearly or work as efficiently, and our immune systems function at only a fraction of their capability. We attempt to make up for these deficiencies with vitamins, medicines, vaccinations and protein shakes. But unfortunately, even with our breakthrough scientific achievements, people still get sick and die.

A fallen environment means that genetic defects get passed down from our parents. It also means that not everything comes together as it should in the womb. As fallen copies of fallen copies, people are born with certain disabilities and differences that are of no fault or choice of their own.

Finally, the realities of our fallen world influence envy, greed and fear. With a limited supply of resources, some have more than enough and some do not. Many who have enough crave to have more. Many who do not have hate those who do. Some of the most cruel, wicked and prejudiced ways we treat each other—not to mention, the most unjust qualities of our governmental, financial and corporate systems—are consequences of the fallen world in which we live.

Reason 2: The Natural Consequences of Personal Sin

While many of the troubles we face have nothing to do with any choice of our own, sadly, some of them do. As we explored in the previous chapter, though we are no longer defined by our sin, the truth is that we still commit sins. And these sins have natural consequences.

I know that sin is explained in many ways by many people, but most basically, according to Scripture, *sin* means "to miss the mark" of God's will.[1] While I certainly do not mean to make light of it, I will use another car illustration to help you understand what it means to sin and how it affects you.

Imagine that you bought a sports car that calls for 93 octane premium gas. To save money, however, you go against the manufacturer's instructions and fill the tank of your hot rod with 87 octane gas. Each time you do this, you have failed to meet the maker's will for that car. Essentially, it could be said that you have sinned against the manufacturer.

You might argue that the car will run on regular gas, and that may be true. But you must trust that the manufacturer did not give those instructions to make you pay more money for your gas or to make your life more difficult. No, the manufacturer knows what its vehicle needs for optimal performance. Though it could run on less, there may be natural consequences to missing the standards of the manufacturer, such as diminished fuel economy, eventual engine damage, or as I personally experienced with my car, a foul, rotten-egg smell coming from the exhaust.

As our Maker, God knows what is best for us to thrive fully in this world that He created. For this reason, He outlined instructions that are found throughout the Bible. Though we might not understand every one of His instructions, we must trust that He has set them forth for our benefit and protection. Each time we fail to follow what He has outlined, even if only slightly, we miss the mark of His best. We will, therefore, experience the natural consequences of it, such as minimal performance or damage to ourselves or others. Eating too much or too little, for example, will have an adverse effect on your health. Spending beyond your means may bring short-term or long-term financial peril. Substance abuse may destroy relationships, careers, opportunities and more. But here again, it is important to realize that none of these tragic and sometimes lasting experiences come from the temper of our Maker. They are simply the natural consequences of missing the mark of His best.

Reason 3: Spiritual Warfare

The final reason for hardships or attacks might not have anything to do with sin. The enemy can somehow perceive God's plan for your life, and he is doing his best to frustrate it. This is called spiritual warfare.

In order not to provoke any paranoia, I must be clear that the enemy is not all-knowing. Only God knows the future and the exact plans He has for you. Still, the devil has been around long enough to identify God's hand on someone. He can see gifts and talents and can hear and read words. Perhaps, as was in the case of Job, the devil is privy to information that we do not yet know. Whatever the case, as soon as the enemy perceives God's plan, he prepares a plot to foil it.

Through my years in ministry, I have recognized that the enemy's attacks usually relate directly to how God intends to use someone in his or her future. This is true at any age, but especially in childhood. Some of the most influential people that I know of were either once victims of tragedy and trauma or had to work through significant personal weaknesses or disabilities.

I think of the early troubles I encountered in my life. While I am fortunate that I never suffered any kind of abuse or tragedy, I see the enemy's fingerprints on the rejection I faced in my youth and the temptations of my early adult years. They seemed targeted uniquely to silence my voice with insecurity and to disqualify me with shame.

What about you? What unfortunate experiences did you go through? What difficulties, trials or struggles do you face today? Can you place them inside one of the three reasons we just explored? Perhaps what has happened around you or to you is the unfortunate reality of living in a fallen world. Maybe your trials are the natural consequences of a mistake or failure. It is possible they are part of the enemy's plot to thwart God's plan for your life. They could be products of a mixture of all three. It does not matter. None of those reflect God's punishment or are reasons to be ashamed or written off. But whether directly or indirectly, they are all the works of the enemy, which means they are all the very reason Jesus came.

Love versus Law

The timeline of the Old Testament spans about the first four thousand years of human history. That is four thousand years of fallen, broken people who are striving for peace with God, trying to earn His blessings and performing in ways they hoped would avert His punishment. But despite their best efforts, none of it worked to keep them on the straight and narrow or at peace with God.

After watching His people being burdened by law and motivated by fear for millennia, God looked down upon His once-perfect, far-fallen creation. He saw a people in darkness who were drudging through brokenness. He observed the pain of sicknesses, disabilities and disorders, the wounds of failed relationships and separated families, and the shame of promiscuity and regrettable acts. He looked upon a sad state of things He did not set in motion that were under the grip of the enemy. God knew that people were powerless to do anything about it on their own, so He implemented His plan to do it for them.

Into a wrecked world, God sent His only Son, Jesus, to be born as flesh with all its limits. While on earth for a mere 33 years, Jesus corrected all the skewed views of God. His ministry of doing good demonstrated that the Father is not condemning but forgiving, not hating but unconditionally loving, not afflicting but healing, not oppressing but free- ing (see Acts 10:38). Then in His greatest act to destroy the chief work of the enemy, Jesus hung on the cross, enduring wave upon wave of God's wrath. In doing so, Jesus ended God's anger forever, established a new covenant of peace with His people and made possible what the Father always desired—to be God with us.

Ultimately, from Old Testament to New, the Bible tells the story of how love did in 33 years what law and legalism could not do in four thousand. It is love that really saved, delivered and healed God's people. And it is love that not only gave humankind access to intimate relationships with the Father, but beckons each of us back to Him in our times of trouble, mistakes and spiritual warfare.

Whatever you face today for whatever reason, know that God is not waiting to tell you off. He is waiting for you to draw near to hear, "I love you. Let's do this together." Be it a minute ago, a day ago, or decades ago—whatever happened to you or in whatever way you blew it—do not delay taking it to the throne of grace in prayer. You will find God waiting with a smile and an embrace.

Renew your mind to this shame-busting truth: God is good, and He greatly loves you. I recognize that it is one thing to hear He loves you, and it is another thing entirely to experience it and say, "God loves *me*!" That is why we are headed next for a meeting with God's love.

Speak It!

Though the circumstances of my past or present might not be good, I know that God is good, and I am good with Him. Because of Jesus, I do not fear God's anger or punishment, but I live at peace with Him every day.

Questions for Personal Reflection

1. What events in your past or present do you believe were the result of God's anger or punishment for something you have done?

2. How has the lie that God is punishing you affected your relationship with Him negatively?

3. With the three reasons in mind of why bad things happen, how might you reconsider the source of your grief, pain and suffering, or the tragic events in the world?

4. Is there any area of your life in which you are missing the mark of God's best for you? Take time now to acknowledge it to God and ask Him to sever its influence on you.

5. How does knowing that God is not mad at you change how you will react to future troubles and pain?

7

"You are unlovable."

In college, I enlisted myself in the "holiness police." I somehow thought it was my job to ensure that my friends were living up to some biblical standard, at least as I saw it. My enforcement was a disapproving glance or a corrective word whenever I heard that they ate, drank or did something "unholy." Not surprisingly, this was not exactly an effective way to win friends and influence people!

Looking back, I see that my hard, legalistic heart was the result of a shallow understanding of God's love. For years, I thought that the concept was elementary. I believed that explanation was something necessary only for those new to the faith but not a message that needed much repeating. I would get intensely frustrated when the pastor of the megachurch I attended gave yet another sermon about God's love.

"Can't we get on with this?" I commonly complained to some of my friends. "There are so many deeper principles of the faith that God's people need to understand." I thought teachings on healing, deliverance, fasting and praying in the Spirit, for example, would serve people far greater than a generic love message.

I wince when I recall the arrogance of my early- to mid-twenties. Deep down, there was much about me that I believed was unlovable. I was shackled internally by a host of insecurities and fears, so I minimized my faith to a collection of self-help principles. I think that is why I cared so much about the "deeper things." They each have their place, but during the holiness-police phase of my life, they were tools to help me "get right" with God. Until they did not.

By my late twenties, all the super-spiritual solutions in the books were not accomplishing what I thought they would. That is when, feeling particularly broken by reminders of my every mistake and undesired quality, I made that cry to God, "What more do I need to do?" The fundamental answer, which came through a journey, was to go back to that elementary message: God loves you.

What I found on my journey is that God's love is anything but basic. Truly, when you finally meet it in all its wonder, it becomes the most profound, healing, delivering and transformative message ever! One that, for all the reasons you are about to see, is ironically now a message I cannot get enough of.

The Source of Love

As I pray with people, I frequently hear, "Kyle, it's easy for me to believe, 'God loves you,' but I can't seem to grasp, 'God loves me.'" When I ask them why, the answer comes down to the reality that people live with themselves. In other words, they are intimately aware of all the reasons that they suppose God should not or could not love them.

Ultimately, the reason we cannot grasp God's love for us has to do with a skewed view of His love that we have adopted from the world. From either observation, experience or some legalistic demonstration of it, many understand love as a quality that is based upon something temporal, and thus, is here today and gone tomorrow. They have come to believe that if they look good enough, achieve enough or behave well enough that they will be loved. If they do not, then they will not.

Regardless of whether your concept of God's love was influenced by a person, an experience or an institution, any misconstrued definition of it is really the devil's doing. He knows that the certainty of God's love is the bedrock of a relationship with Him. That is why he uses every opportunity to convince you that it is not possible for God to love someone like you.

But every argument that the enemy makes to that end is a lie. The truth is that it is impossible for God *not* to love you. You see, God does not choose whether or not He will apply His love. Love is not something that God does, because love is who He is: "God is love, and all who live in love live in God, and God lives in them" (1 John 4:16).

If you wonder how it is possible for God to love without conditions or how He can love people who do not love Him back, this is it. May you have the grace to grasp even a bit of the magnitude of what this means for you! Because God is love, He is not weighing your good works against your mess ups to see if the scale tips in favor of you being worthy of love today. The truth that we can only teeter along the edges of understanding is that God cannot help but love because He is love.

I suspect that God knew our finite minds could not comprehend completely a limitless love as this. That is why He embodied the mystery of it in flesh. From His birth to His resurrection, everything that Jesus did modeled what love really is. When He spoke to the unspeakables, touched the untouchables, forgave the unforgivables and used the unusables, He revealed real love so radical that it killed Him. Literally. Jesus' love was so countercultural and otherworldly that the world could not put up with it.

I could fill the rest of this book with stories of Jesus' interactions with people, and the stories would hardly scratch the surface of how they each demonstrate aspects of God's love. That is why the apostle Paul wrote that the love of Christ is too great to understand fully (see Ephesians 3:19). We may never grasp completely a love that knows no boundaries—at least on this side of eternity—but we can meet it. We can be changed by it. Just as one unlikely woman who was smack dab in the midst of her shame was changed. Let's join her meeting with God's love.

The Meeting with God's Love

The story begins in the countryside of Judea. Wrapping up some time with His cousin John, Jesus made plans to return to Galilee. But there was a problem. Judea is in southern Israel. Galilee is in northern Israel. Sandwiched between the two is forty miles of a heathenville known as Samaria.

In order to understand the conundrum Jesus faced, you have to know a bit of history. In the centuries before Jesus, distrust between His fellow Jews and the Samaritans had grown to all-out hatred. To simplify a long, complicated story, the Samaritans were descendants of Israelites who had intermarried with other races. Consequently, they became known to the Jews as half-breeds, who had adopted worldly ways and strayed from pure doctrine. By the time of Christ, His fellow Jews considered the Samaritans too dirty and too different to be looked upon or spoken to, much less to be considered lovable by God.

To avoid being contaminated by such people, it is believed that some Jews who needed to get from Judea to Galilee would take extra days to go around Samaria. But not Jesus. The Bible is sure to make note that "He had to go through Samaria on the way" (John 4:4).

He *had* to. I do not think the necessity had anything to do with a time crunch. I am convinced that the reason He went through Samaria had everything to do with the central reason He was sent into our world: to reveal the Father's love.

Along Jesus' journey the Bible records, "he came to the Samaritan village of Sychar" (verse 5), where there was a historically known well. While passing through, He begins to feel the weight of His humanity, and He needs a break, which He takes at the well around noontime. But Jesus does not rest for long. Shortly into His respite, a lone woman arrives to draw water. That is when Jesus does the unthinkable, at least for a Jewish man. He asks her for a drink (see verses 6–7).

I have to pause here to highlight the enormity of what just happened. Not only did Jesus not avoid the region of Samaria, but He also spent time in one of its cities. While there, He did something extremely counter to His own religious system—He asked a Samaritan woman for a drink! In doing so, he committed a double no-no. First, He interacted with a Samaritan. Second, He spoke to a woman in public. Both were forbidden by His own people.

The Bible records the woman's disbelief. I imagine her head held low in insecurity, eyes pinging from side to side careful not to make eye contact with Jesus. "You are a Jew, and I am a Samaritan woman," she timidly acknowledged (verse 9). Then, perhaps looking up with trepidation and meeting His eyes for the first time, she wondered aloud, "Why are you asking me for a drink?" Jesus' response is as radical as everything He has done up to this point: "If you only knew the gift God has for you and who you are speaking to, you would ask me, and I would give you living water" (verse 10).

Far removed from their culture, I am not sure we can appreciate the crime it was for a Jewish rabbi to ask a Samaritan woman for something, much less suggest that God had a gift for her. But this is love! In barely a minute of interaction, Jesus took a wrecking ball to everything the highest scholars of His religion believed about God's love. He modeled that God's love knows no bigotry; it knows no boundaries. God loves the outcasts, the rejects, the ones whom the religious world deems too dirty or too different. But not only does God love them, He goes out of His way to pursue them with the offer of a gift.

Do you relate to the Samaritan woman? Has something about your past, your struggles or your family history been used by people—maybe even church people—to define you as a certain kind of person who is unlovable by God or unwelcome in the Body of Christ? Have you been made to feel that you are too dirty or too different to be of any value?

If that is you, please consider what we witnessed from Jesus. He does not base His love for you upon where you came from or where you are right now. His love is not hinged upon you being part of the right group, having perfect theology or appearing cleaned up enough to deserve it. No, you are worth everything to God because inside of you is a treasure, His image. Yes, the Bible reveals that you were made in God's image. And though the experiences of life may have covered that image with layer upon layer of shame and struggle, it is still there. That is reason enough for why God loves you unconditionally. But there is so much more.

The Place of God's Love

Sometimes it is easy to forget that the conveniences we come to expect today did not exist one hundred years ago, let alone in the first century. Indoor plumbing with running water is one of them. That is why homes were frequently built around community wells that people walked to every day. Their walk for water was not a casual stroll, though. It could be quite an arduous event of balancing buckets for a half mile or more.

For most, the added weight of filled-to-the-brim water jars would have been enough to tire them out. But imagine making such a hike on one of the scorching-hot days typical of that region. This walk would not have been made on concrete wearing Nikes, but on rocky, dusty roads, barefoot or in sandals. It certainly does not sound fun to me. It was not to them, either, which is why they attempted to lessen the burden by making the journey in the cool of the morning or evening. With everyone making their trip at the same time, the community well became quite the social hotspot. I am sure that it was a hotspot for gossip, too.

But Jesus met the woman at the well around noontime. Why would she make such a difficult journey at the hottest time of the day? Did she get a late start to her morning?

Perhaps a surprise delayed her journey? No. This was not a one-time occurrence. The woman purposefully chose the worst time of day to avoid the crowds because she was ashamed.

Understand that the scandal of Jesus' meeting is not only that He interacted with a Samaritan woman, but that He interacted with an outcast who had a sordid history of promiscuity and a string of failed relationships. In a small village of possibly only a few hundred people, you can bet she had a reputation. Thus, scheduling her daily water collection at noontime was the best way for her to avoid catching the judgmental glances or cruel whispers of those who deemed themselves much holier. It was the best way for her to hide in shame.

Do you ever hide to avoid people to escape their judgment or rejection? Hiding is the primal effect of shame. It is what caused Adam and Eve to hide from God in the bushes. It is what keeps us isolated from people, especially "God's people."

Having a media ministry, I see it all the time. People who would never step foot inside a church, for the same reason the woman went to the well at noontime, tune in to my broadcasts. Behind a screen, they do not feel as if they stick out in the midst of what they perceive is a cookie-cutter congregation of perfect people. Behind a screen, nobody is there to judge them for the whys: why their marriage failed, why they are still single, why they do not have children, why they are still sick, why they do not have a job and so on.

To be fair, I do not think most others are sizing up our situations as we fear that they are, but it doesn't matter. Shame is the belief that something in our lives makes us wrong, and we fear that all anyone sees is that one reason we do not fit in. And in the middle of a crowd, it can feel as if all eyes are on us.

Going back to the story, imagine the surprise and fear the woman must have felt when she came upon a Jewish man—the most judgmental of them all—in the place of her hiding. But this was no accidental encounter. Jesus did not get winded suddenly and decide to catch His breath the moment this outcast woman happened to arrive. No, this meeting was the result of a pursuit. Jesus went right into the place of her hiding—the place where she was expecting the most judgment—to give her value, to show her mercy and to demonstrate God's unconditional love.

Perhaps you picked up this book in the midst of your worst place. Maybe you are reading these words at the height of a situation you are not proud of, or while you are overwhelmed with a feeling that condemns you. Whatever the case, you must know that you did not stumble here out of happenstance. This moment was scheduled by your heavenly Father who pursued you here! As He did for the woman at the well, Jesus waited patiently for you to read this very sentence in which He says, "You aren't wrong to Me. I don't judge you. I don't condemn you. Where you are, as you are—you are valuable to Me."

The Purpose of God's Love

Fresh from Jesus' request for a drink and His offer of a gift, the woman experiences enough boldness within her to carry on some small talk with Him. At least, that is how I see what happens next. Jesus offered her living water. Who could understand what He meant? She didn't. She misunderstood and thought that Jesus referred to some more expensive water found deeper in the well. Maybe Fiji instead of Dasani.

All joking aside, her misunderstanding continues for a few minutes more until He gets personal.

"Go and get your husband" (verse 16). Remember, Jesus is God, which means He is all-knowing.

He certainly was not surprised when she confessed, "I don't have a husband" (verse 17).

To this, Jesus replied, "You're right! You don't have a husband—for you have had five husbands, and you aren't even married to the man you're living with now" (verse 18).

When I read this years ago with my shallow understanding of God's love, Jesus' words almost seemed condemning. It felt as if Jesus sneered, "Ah ha! I caught you in a lie!" But I no longer think that was His tone. I imagine that as she flinched from the truth and looked down in shame, Jesus stepped in front of her, placed His hands tenderly on the sides of her shoulders, and then ducked His head down to meet hers as if to coerce her to look up at Him. I see the two face-to-face just inches apart. She, staring at Him with bated breath and wondering what He might say, and He with a furrowed brow and half smile of compassion connecting His eyes with hers in a way that gently expressed, "I know all about you. And it's okay."

Whatever really happened, the woman did not retreat like an abused animal. She drew nearer and grew bolder in order to ask Him some questions. Jesus obliged for a minute, but then cut to the quick to get to the purpose of their meeting: His introduction. "I AM the Messiah" (verse 26).

Let's reflect upon everything that transpired so far. Jesus met this outcast Samaritan woman in a place she did not want to be seen. Then He called out the source of her shame. Finally, by introducing Himself to her as the Messiah, He essentially assured her, "I know the worst about you, but that doesn't change My mind about you. I am your God, and I want you in My family."

Along my journey to meet God's love, I remember Him comforting me in a similar way. It happened when I finally got real about some problems in my life that I verbalized in prayer to Him. Listing these issues to God, some for the very first time aloud, I felt fear arise in me from a thought: *Now that God knows the worst about me, maybe He cannot use me!*

It seems that God was ready for this reaction, because I was led immediately to a Scripture verse: "Even before he made the world, God loved us and chose us in Christ to be holy and without fault in his eyes" (Ephesians 1:4).

In the light of my fear, this familiar verse took on a deep, new meaning. God used it to say, *Kyle, you are no surprise to me. I knew all this when I called you, and yet I still called you.*

I invite you to take in all that this verse means for you, too. As much as it is humanly possible to comprehend, please receive the truth that God knew you long before He made you. Long before He made the world. Incomprehensibly, before you were news to your parents, God knew you—all about you. Yet despite knowing all the ways you would fall short and all the messes you would make in this life, He still chose to bring you into existence so that one day He could introduce Himself.

As Jesus conveyed to the woman at the well, and as He comforted me, He is whispering to you, *You are no surprise to Me! I know all about you. I loved you before you were made. I loved you through the messes you made. I love you in this very moment. I am Your God, and I want you in My family.*

No Greater Love

In the end, the Samaritan woman is so stunned by her inter-action with Jesus that she completely abandoned the reason that she came to the well in the first place. Dropping her water jar, she wasted no time running back to the village to tell everyone, "Come and see a man who told me every-thing I ever did! Could he possibly be the Messiah?" (John 4:29).

Do you get the picture? This woman who came to the well at an inconvenient time of day so that she did not have to face anyone from her village now suddenly faced everyone with boldness. A meeting with God's love changed her! She was loved out of shame, out of the belief that her past made her an outcast and out of the fear that someone like her could not be in God's family. But this was not a random demonstration of love. No, the love that Jesus showed in the story of the Samaritan woman is representative of every-thing He did.

I tremble from a flood of awe over what I am about to write. When God took on human flesh and entered our world, He did not lecture people into submission with dos and don'ts. He never once belittled with condemnation or wrote any struggler out of the faith. Instead, in demonstrat-ing the purest kind of love, He walked alongside flawed, broken people and entered their battles with them, offering a hand up and a way out. With no guarantee they would ever love Him back, nor with any effort or promise to change their ways, Jesus laid down His life so that broken, flawed people could be brought into the family of their perfect Creator. If you need a vision of real love, it is this: "While we were still sinners, Christ died for us" (Romans 5:8 ESV).

What a love! In the place of our brokenness and knowing the worst about us before we ever had a chance to love Him back or prove anything to Him, Jesus sacrificed Himself to prove His love for us. What could ever come between the kind of love that is unconditionally willing to die for someone? The Bible boasts that nothing has that kind of power (see Romans 8:38). No person. No past. No battle. Nothing.

A Love Letter from the Lord

As you continue through this book, everything you have discovered so far is foundational to accepting the truths in the pages ahead. Knowing you are right with God and loved unconditionally by Him are paramount for accepting His forgiveness for your past regrets and present struggles. We will address that next.

Before we move on, there is something I want to leave you with. It is something heartfelt and healing. One day as I sensed that He wanted to speak, I sat on my couch and opened my phone's notes app to get down whatever He had to say. What I received is a love letter from the Lord that was addressed to *you*. Here is what it reads:

> *My Child,*
> *Before you took your first innocent breath in this temporary home, and before the news of your coming was ever known—before you were formed—I knew you. I knew all about you, and I loved you.*
> *You were always my idea. When I considered the uniqueness you would bring and what it would offer*

My world, I made a choice to orchestrate your existence. So I spoke, "Let there be you." And I am happy I did.

Every feature and shape, the precise way your face creases when you smile (oh, how I love that smile), the sound of your laugh and the passions you pursue—those are not quirks, they are qualities. Qualities I crafted to make you, you.

But what I love the most—why I made that consequential choice to bring you to life—is far more than anything you can do. It is the sound of your voice. Every word you confide. Every struggle you share. Every mess you confess. I look forward to those precious, tender moments when our hearts connect.

My child, I love you. And all the words in a million love letters cannot adequately express what that means. You will find out more in time. But for now, know that there is nothing you can do to change My mind. I love you. And I am so glad you are here with Me.

Love,
Your Father, God

Speak It!

Nothing in my past or present can separate me from the love of God who made me in His image and sent His Son to die for me. I am not only lovable to God, but I am loved deeply by Him every day . . . just as I am.

Questions for Personal Reflection

1. What in, around or about your life has kept you from believing that God could completely love you as you are?

2. What does it mean to you to be made in God's image? How could this revelation change the way you see yourself?

3. Imagine Jesus showing up at your "well" at noon—in the place of your deepest regret, struggle or embarrassment. Knowing His character, what do you think Jesus would tell you in these moments?

4. In light of the fact that Jesus treated the Samaritan woman with kindness and respect even though He knew everything about her, how do you think He would treat you even though He knows everything about you?

5. After this chapter, has your view of God's love changed? In what ways? How will it affect your life?

8

LIE:

"You cannot be forgiven."

"Look what you've done!" Those are the words I heard barely one month into stepping into my own ministry. For years, I had worked behind-the-scenes for other ministries climbing the ladder of leadership. Now nearing my thirties, I sensed God calling me to establish something new.

Typically, anything new is met with resistance—especially if it is of any spiritual significance. So I knew that launching something like this would not be a cake walk. But I was not expecting the sudden onslaught of reminders of my every sin since potty training!

For a week, my mind was the object of accusations that beat me to tears. These accusations came from reminders of the sins of my adult life—the things I had done after I had become a Christian. I was burdened by the weight of shame to the point that I almost walked away from God's call. I believed that someone like me could not be used by Him.

Added to all the accusations were my own questions. By this time, I had been a born-again, made-new Christian for more than a decade. Why were my past sins being brought up again? Why were the reminders of them still so condemning? The accusations that week made me wonder if I was not really forgiven by God. Or worse, had I committed sins that could not be forgiven? These questions haunted me as much as the reminders themselves.

Can you relate? Since I shared this story in my first book, I have heard from many who do. Some confess, "Kyle, I can't see how God could forgive me after the things I've done." Others lament, "Even though I've asked Him countless times, I don't feel forgiven!"

If you feel something similar, please know that you are far from alone. I hosted an online poll that asked, "How would you describe your current experience with forgiveness?" A whopping 65 percent of Christians admitted they cannot accept it, either from God, themselves or both. While that is an unscientific poll, I found it reflects accurately what I have seen in ministry. Many of the battles people have with themselves (and others) are rooted in a lie that they cannot be forgiven.

When You Were Forgiven

To help silence the accusations and questions I faced that week, God led me back to the foundation of forgiveness. While lying prostrate on my couch, He gave me a picture of the moment that Jesus paid for our sins on the cross. It was raw. It was gruesome. But it was so healing!

What I witnessed that morning with my mind's eye is the reality of what the apostle Paul wrote regarding the effect of the cross. It is the when and where of your forgiveness, too, which is why I want to unpack it throughout this chapter. Paul began, "You were dead because of your sins and because your sinful nature was not yet cut away" (Colossians 2:13).

We have already spent time understanding the position we were in before salvation. But here again, Paul described the state that required Jesus' radical sacrifice. Our sins made us dead, incapable of pleasing God ourselves, and unable to be in relationship with Him on our own merit. But Paul does not linger here long, for there is good news to get to: "Then God made you alive with Christ, for he forgave all our sins" (verse 13).

What Paul described is how your supernatural change in identity happened. He illustrated it like a surgery in which God cut out your sin nature. Think of it like a cancerous tumor. Before Jesus, this impure thing in you consumed your thoughts, dictated your behaviors and controlled your life. It was your identity. And as identities do, it incited issues in all your relationships. Most importantly, though, it stood between you and God.

Like a cancer, the sin nature intends to spread and take over. That is why it could not be merely treated and minimized. It had to be utterly cut out. And that is exactly what God did. In the split second after you believed in Jesus, God removed what was killing you. He did that so that you could have an unending, abundant life in Christ.

Calling this great news hardly does it justice! It describes the "re-geneing" process that we explored back in chapter 5. But I do not want you to miss the way Paul summarized how all of this happens, because it is of utmost importance to what we are talking about. He boils the entire process down to "for [God] forgave all our sins."

I do not mean to be cheeky, but *all* means all. Paul added no qualifiers, such as "from the past" or "up to the point of salvation." He gives no indication of certain kinds or levels of sins that are not included. Rather, Paul boasted that all our sins are forgiven. This means past, present and future. In order for God to do what was necessary to give us life, He had to forgive every sin from any time. If there was even one that retained its power, then you would still be defined by sin and separated from God.

In Christ, no sin has the power to identify you, separate you from God or condemn you anymore. At the cross, Jesus took that power away. Paul puts it in no uncertain terms: "[Jesus] canceled the record of the charges against us and took it away by nailing it to the cross" (verse 14).

Friend, your sins—past, present and future—were forgiven once and for all because of Jesus' sacrifice on the cross. Anything less would have left the job incomplete. This forgiveness of all your sins was applied to you the instant you believed that Jesus did it. I know that may seem too simple. The devil definitely wants you to believe it is. That is why he always insists that there has to be more that you have to do, more that you have to know and more that you have to feel sorry about. But the Gospel is called Good News for the very fact that the forgiveness of sins was a done deal at the cross and then forever applied to you upon your belief.

What Is Forgiveness, Anyway?

As I counsel people who have a difficult time accepting that they are forgiven, I have found that the struggle is often rooted in a misconception about what God's forgiveness really is. Most think of it in an intangible way that is nothing more than Him accepting an apology. After they say, "I'm sorry, Lord," but then hear or feel nothing, they are left wondering, *Did it really happen?*

If this is the extent of what we think God's forgiveness is, it is no wonder we cannot receive it. God's forgiveness is not merely Him accepting a verbal apology, but it is a full pardon of a crime. That is blunt, but it is true. The Bible describes sin as breaking a law that has to be paid by a penalty such as a fine or a sentence.

The Old Testament is filled with laws, many of which we have all broken, some every day. Most famous are the Ten Commandments given by God to Moses on stone tablets. These include instructions such as honor your father and mother, do not steal and do not lie (see Exodus 20:3–17). Unknown to most, the Law was actually comprised of many more commandments—613, to be exact.[1] That is 613 potential ways to fail and reasons to be penalized. No human could ever abide by them all. Again, that is why God sent Jesus.

To put this into a modern context, imagine standing trial for breaking any one of these laws. In the courtroom, there are three primary parties: the defendant, you; the accuser, the devil; the Judge, God. The problem is that in this trial, there is no question of the verdict. The devil does not have to do much work to prove your guilt. All he really does is detail what you did and which law you broke.

As the accuser rests his case, you brace for judgment. Staring at the floor, you take deep breaths to try to slow your racing heart. But it beats all the faster knowing that the book is about to be thrown at you. For some reason, seeing your trepidation gives the accuser a sinister kind of pleasure. You catch his smirk as the Judge postures Himself for the ruling.

Before He begins, however, the Judge asks, "Do you have any final words you'd like to say?" And you do.

Looking up into the eyes of Justice, your voice quivers with contrition. "Your Honor, I'm so sorry!" What you confessed is heartfelt. Nobody doubts it, not even the accuser. Even the Judge nods to accept your apology. But justice would not be served by only accepting an apology. A penalty still has to be paid.

Locking His eyes on yours without a blink, the Judge takes a breath, purses His lips and then opens His mouth to speak. Suddenly, a commotion arises from the back of the courtroom. A seemingly desperate man lunges forward to approach the bench.

Attempting to catch his breath, he pleads, "Your honor, your honor! I'll pay this penalty!"

The courtroom gasps. You freeze in unbelief. This disheveled-looking man you do not yet know offered to take what you deserve.

The accuser counters in anger, "No, no, no! The defendant has to pay!" But the sentence is not up to him. It is up to the Judge, and His face turns from contemplative to curiously pleased. Before He turns back to you, He offers the man a wink as if He knows Him, almost as if He has been waiting for this moment to happen all along.

"Do you accept this man's offer?" the Judge questions you. Like a bobblehead just after a bump, your head bounces up and down in agreement.

"Yes, yes, yes! I accept!" you gush with gratitude.

"It's final then," the Judge declares. "This man takes your penalty. You are free!"

The accuser storms out of the courtroom shouting, "I'll never accept this!" And he never does. He returns from time to time with reminders of old failures and new accusations. But his best evidence cannot accomplish what it once did. For you were saved and freed by grace, and that judgment remains on the books forever, never needing to be repeated.

The desperate man who came running to save you from the sentence the law required is no mere man. He is Jesus. Every beating, thrashing and broken bone He endured on the cross was Him taking accountability and paying the punishment for your crimes. This is when and how, as Colossians assures, the charges against you were canceled. The Judge's declaration is God's forgiveness, which was given to you the moment you said, "Yes, Jesus, I accept what You did for me."

Are There Unforgivable Sins?

To bolster the feeling of not being forgiven, the enemy twists Scripture so that people read it to believe that certain sins are unforgivable. The accuser knows the Law far better than any of us, and he will spin it to fit whatever narrative leaves us the most hopeless.

That is what happened to a man who wrote to me a few years ago. Reacting to a fear that had been incited suddenly in him by a single passage from the Bible, he frantically wrote, "Kyle, I'm scared. It seems that I have committed an unforgivable sin. I'm afraid God doesn't love me! I'm afraid I won't go to heaven!"

Reading the first couple of sentences of his email, I was initially perplexed. What could have possibly given him the idea that there is a sin that can't be forgiven? But as I kept reading his worried words, he mentioned some verses the enemy loves to twist:

[Don't you know] that the unrighteous shall not inherit the kingdom of God? Be not deceived: neither fornicators, nor idolaters, nor adulterers, nor effeminate, nor abusers of themselves with mankind, nor thieves, nor covetous, nor drunkards, nor revilers, nor extortioners, shall inherit the kingdom of God.

1 Corinthians 6:9–10 KJV

Without any other context, it is easy to see why we might fear that we have done something that disqualifies us from God's Kingdom. After all, this list describes kinds of people who do things that we have all done at some level.

But that is just it—it describes kinds of people. This is not a list of sins, nor is it a list of experiences. It is a list of identities.

Is it true that Christians still engage in some of what these identities are known for? Sadly, yes. The reality is that Christians still make some colossal mistakes. This is why, as I explained in chapter 6, that the Bible never assures that sin is dead. It assures, instead, that sin's ability to separate us from God is dead (see Romans 6:6).

A principle of studying the Bible that I was fortunate enough to learn early in my faith is that Scripture interprets Scripture. In a book the size of the Bible, all kinds of wacky beliefs could be supported if you only read a verse here or there. But in instances when you are confused about what the Bible means or to whom it is speaking, it is best to interpret it based upon what you know from other verses. This is especially crucial for understanding 1 Corinthians 6:9–10.

You see, while the passage lists people who are unrighteous, we know from plenty of other verses that it cannot be talking about Christians. The Bible is clear that

126

Christians have been declared righteous (2 Corinthians 5:21). What follows after the list affirms this all the more. "And such were some of you: but [you] are washed, but [you] are sanctified, but [you] are justified in the name of the Lord Jesus, and by the Spirit of our God" (1 Corinthians 6:11 KJV).

I am not sure how the Bible could be more clear when it says such were some of you—but Jesus. Because of His finished work, you are clean, set apart by God (sanctified) and made as if you have never sinned (justified).

This single verse is so rich! While I do not want to over-complicate it, there is even more behind this verse. If you will allow me to go a bit deeper, I would love to explain. What we miss in our English translations are the nuances of the original Greek. In this case, the modern reader sees the word *are* and thinks present tense, which is certainly the case. Christians are presently clean, set apart and justified. But in the Greek language, there is more meaning. The word *are* is an aorist verb, which refers to something that happened in the past but has no ending or expiration. Accordingly, the truth that this verse conveys is that you were forgiven at the moment of your salvation, *and* you will continue to be forgiven (past, present and future). Yes, because you are in Christ, nothing can cause you to be unclean. Nothing can stop you from being set apart by God. Nothing can stop God from looking at you as if you never sinned.

Let this truth absorb into your soul. There is not one sin that can be named for which Jesus did not die. The only experience that is unpardonable is unbelief. The reason is straightforward. God cannot credit Jesus' payment to your charges if you do not believe He did it and say yes to accept it. But if you have placed your faith in Christ sincerely, then be assured that you are and will continue to be forgiven.

The Faithfulness of Forgiveness

"But Kyle," one lady wrote, "I keep repeating the same things over and over. I've asked God for forgiveness only to fail to the same ole, same ole, again and again." To be sure, she was not happy about her failures. But after years of battling things that she hates, the woman wondered to me, "Did God stop forgiving me? Will He stop forgiving me?"

It is human to think of everything in limited supply. Nothing material lasts forever. Money gets spent. Energy gets exhausted. Inventory goes out of stock. We imagine mistakenly that God's forgiveness is the same. But all throughout the Bible, God's forgiveness is never described in ways that suggest it is a resource that could ever be depleted. No, Scripture refers to it beautifully as endless and faithful: "But if we confess our sins to him, he is faithful and just to forgive us our sins and to cleanse us from all wickedness" (1 John 1:9).

Some years ago, God led me to see the reflection of this truth in the physics of His creation. One evening as I was walking along the shoreline of a beach not far from where I lived, I saw beyond the stunning watercolor-looking sunset and emerald sea into an even more stunning spiritual illustration.

Imagine it with me. Watch the waves that crash upon the shore turning into a layer of suds that wash over the sand and then recede back into the sea. This happens over again and again. They are faithful. As people walk by and leave their footprints in the sand, the waves are faithful to remove them. Sandcastles are almost instantly dissolved. Debris washes away with every wave.

When I saw this, I recognized that the sand represents the slate of our lives. All the tracks, graffiti and rubble are symbolic of the sin, struggle and mess we make in our lives. With this epiphany, I stooped down and ran my fingers through the sand and added my own mess to it. Finally, with my index finger, I wrote the word *sin*.

Standing back up, I only had a few seconds before what I knew would happen. But I had to see it with my own eyes. Sure enough, those faithful waves washed over my mess. And as they pulled away, it was as if the sand had been washed clean. There was not a trace left of anything I had done. The big *sin* in the sand was gone, too. I did it all a few more times, and the waves never failed to make all things new!

This simple act of creation is a beautiful illustration of God's forgiveness. At the moment of your salvation, the waves of God's grace crashed over the shore of your life and left no trace of what was formerly there. Indeed, your past was washed away. But that was not the end of your forgiveness. No, God's grace is always there to keep you clean. As a Christian, no mess is permanent. No sin can stain you. Every time you blow it and go to God in confession, you do so not to beg Him to forgive you once more as if you are on trial yet again. No, you go to God in confession to have your mind renewed to the judgment that still stands. You go to hear Him lovingly remind you, *You are free. You are forgiven. Now, walk in the identity you've been given. You have been made new, made right, made whole and made holy.*

Please understand, the faithfulness of God's forgiveness is not an excuse to do as you please. As we have already explored, sin has natural consequences that are foolish to continue to subject yourself to. But the Christian life is not about living in perpetual sorrow for what God knows you could never live up to in your own willpower. The Christian life is living in the joy of your salvation because of what Jesus did for you.

Feeling Forgiven

When God took me back to the cross that week, it was not because I needed to be forgiven or saved again. I needed to finally understand that the significance of the cross was that I was forgiven once and for all. Envisioning what Jesus did helped me to get God's forgiveness from my head to my heart.

What happened next really made the truth stick with me. *Make a record of your wrongs*, I felt God instruct.

"Do I really need a visible reminder of everything I'm hearing so clearly?" I argued to myself. Still, I was obedient. I took out a pen and paper to list everything for which I felt condemned. It didn't take me long to fill the page. But what was I to do next? Hang the paper on my wall to remain forever conscious of my failures? God cut quickly through my curiosity with the truths that we have been unpacking from Colossians 2:14.

I heard, *I canceled the record of charges against you.* To be sure, none of this was audible, but it was as if thought after thought was being dropped into my head.

Next, I sensed that I was to draw a cross all over that paper until my wrongs were covered with the symbol of what Jesus had done to make me right. But covered was not enough. The cross is not simply a means of covering our sins to get them out of God's sight for a while—that is Old Testament. No, Jesus' work finished them off! As the verse says, the record was canceled and nailed to the cross. Through the realization of what this meant about the list that I held in my hands, God led me to take the final step to be able to visualize it.

Rip it to shreds, He instructed. So that is what I did! I have never experienced something more satisfying! I made one big tear down the center and then dozens more to the remaining pieces until the record of my wrongs was but a heap of confetti on the floor.

It is hard to describe adequately the significance of this moment for me, except to say that I finally felt it. Seeing an illustration of what had happened at the cross—what I had accepted with my belief in Christ—brought a feeling of victory to me that I had never experienced before.

Though I had officially started my ministry about a month earlier, this was the moment that it really began. This process changed everything for me. No longer would I live from a place of hoping God might forgive me or from fear that I had used up the last of His grace. I would live in and minister from the victory and freedom of knowing that nothing exists that can condemn me. That is precisely what the apostle Paul revealed after describing how Jesus canceled the record of our wrongs. "So don't let anyone condemn you," he passionately concluded (Colossians 2:16).

With that pile of shredded paper at my feet, I decided that I would no longer allow any voice from the past, my present struggles, or the enemy to condemn me. I resolved to use the certainty of God's Word to say, "Shut up, devil!"

I do not share this story to suggest that you reenact what I did. While it might be helpful for you to have a visual of your sins being canceled, ultimately, I want you to understand what it brought me to understand. It is a key principle that I have already said in this book: God's Word is more real than what you feel.

The truth is that you will not always feel forgiven. The accuser will return to retry your failures in the courtroom of your mind, which inevitably will sting. But feelings are not facts. God's Word is your ultimate reality. And what it confirms is that as a believer all your sins were forgiven, are forgiven and will continue to be forgiven. When any reminder, feeling or voice tries to tell you otherwise, use God's Word to renew your mind.

This is not, of course, advice that you are to follow only when you feel unforgiven. It is crucial to do when you experience any negative feeling, especially the one we are about to confront—the feeling of fear. Let's shut this one down in the next chapter.

Speak It!

Jesus took the record of my past, present and future sins and nailed it to the cross; therefore, I am no longer condemned or defined by failures, struggles or shortcomings. God has declared me free. I am forgiven!

Questions for Personal Reflection

1. In any healing process, it is important to identify what is causing the issue. What are the specific sins, failures or experiences that make you feel condemned or unforgiven?

2. Have you ever considered that the Bible's assurance that "He forgave all our sins" includes your past, present and future sins? How does this truth have an impact on what you called to mind?

3. How will the guarantee that you are clean, set apart and seen by God as if you never sinned affect your everyday life?

4. How will the revelation of the faithfulness of God's forgiveness change how you relate to God?

5. What are some truths from God's Word that you can use to shut down accusations or feelings of shame?

9

"You should be afraid."

Admittedly, I rarely chronicle my feelings or experiences in a physical journal. Instead, I keep a running list of thoughts, prayers, insights and ideas in my notes app.

But this day was different. It was so monumental that I wanted my thoughts recorded permanently in writing. What looks like it was penned with a nervous hand reads,

> *Dear Journal,*
>
> *You know I don't write in you often enough, but today is a big day. Today is the last day at my job before I step out completely on my own into the unknowns of this ministry God's called me to.*
>
> *I'd be lying if I said I wasn't afraid, mostly of two things: Where will the money come from to sustain both myself and the expenses of the ministry? Will I have enough content to come up with weekly messages?*

The costs are already mounting, and I just can't allow my mind to think too far about it all. Nevertheless, opportunities have presented themselves. Others have given me words that confirm it. You know I can be skeptical of those at times, but I want to believe them, and I will.

So from today, I step out with shaking legs and butterflies in my stomach. But I'm stepping out.

Perhaps parts of that short journal entry are not what you would expect from someone writing a book that has as bold a title as this one. The insecurity, doubt and skepticism on display here might not be a textbook model of faith, but they are real. They are human. And I suspect that you can relate to them.

Less than a day away from losing the stability of a salary and benefits, I did not feel strong when I jotted that on paper. Still, in hindsight, I recognize remarkable growth compared to how I used to react to fear. You see, for over half of my life, fear was a voice that taunted from the sidelines. It was a voice that I always obeyed. It demanded insistently, "Stop! Avoid! Run!"

That is why through at least my early adult years, I was possibly more known for quitting than anything else. I quit my first year of preschool. I quit piano lessons. I quit baseball and basketball. I quit Boy Scouts. I quit band. This list goes on. Either I was afraid to talk to people, afraid that I would fail or afraid that I would be rejected. Fear always convinced me to quit.

What is different between then and today is not that I have somehow convinced fear to stop talking or that I do not feel afraid anymore. The growth I see in my journal entry is that

I stopped being influenced by it. I will show you how to do the same.

Putting Feelings in Their Place

A key to silencing fear is understanding what it is. Fear is a feeling. And as I said in the last chapter, feelings are not facts. That does not mean all emotions are of the devil and should be denied—they just need to be put in their place. God created feelings to be a guide, not a master. Feelings can help you size up a situation or assist you in making a decision. But because they are easily manipulated, they should never be solely depended upon to make a decision.

A few months before writing this book, I attempted a small construction project that reminded me of how deceptive feelings can be. My goal was to build some faux walls inside my house. Since I did not have any experience in building this kind of structure, I requested the assistance of a friend who did.

After collecting all the supplies from the local hardware store, we began the construction by laying a couple of precut two-by-fours on the ground a few inches apart. They each needed to be exactly eight feet long. But upon measuring the first one, we realized the store had not cut it precisely. We took off a couple of inches.

When it came time for the second piece, I got a little impatient. We were working outside as dark clouds and sounds of distant thunder suggested impending rain. Eager to get finished before any wet weather destroyed the project, I wanted to skip the measurement of the second piece. After all, just inches away from the recently cut one, it looked to me to be the exact same size.

While I argued that we move on to save time, my experienced friend insisted we measure. After a few huffs and puffs and at least one eye roll, I relented. Sure enough, my friend was right. Fairly dramatically, actually. The second piece of lumber was not a centimeter or two off. It was a full couple of inches too long.

My feelings had deceived me. Though they had been useful to show that the two pieces were similar, they were not useful to tell me the exact size. For that, I needed the added help of something designed specifically for precise measurement—a measuring tape.

How the Enemy Uses Fear

You might be surprised to know that like other feelings fear can be a useful guide, particularly to protect you from danger. You should feel afraid to place your hand on a scorching-hot burner, to jump out of an airplane without a parachute or to risk all your money on a lottery. That is fear working as God designed it.

But as we explored in chapter 3, the enemy perverts God's good designs to use against us. He uses feelings of fear as one of his most potent means of persuasion. The devil wants fear to be so real to you that the mere existence of a challenge does not just warn of potential danger but also promises the certainty of it. The voice of fear shouting at you might sound something like this:

- "Those bills will turn into bankruptcy."
- "The boss has called the meeting to fire you."
- "Those symptoms are going to kill you."

- "They did not respond to your text because they are mad at you."

In reality, of course, bills rarely mean bankruptcy. A meeting could be called for a million other reasons besides being fired. Despite what certain medical websites might have you believe, symptoms are not a sure death sentence. And there are plenty of other explanations as to why someone might not have responded right away. Perhaps they were busy or did not see your message.

Here again, like the false interpretations of facts that we discussed earlier, the first part of the enemy's argument is based on reality. The latter part is an unknown, which he fills in with worst-case scenarios. That is why psychologists note that lack of information is a leading cause of fear.[1] It is another instance when our fallen minds simply default to "what-can-go-wrong-will-go-wrong" kind of thinking.

But what can go wrong most often does not go wrong. At least, not in the worst ways fear says it will. That is backed up by a handful of scientific studies. One of the more prominent ones that was conducted by Penn State University asked 29 people to write down all the fears they experienced in one month. At the conclusion of the study, the researchers found that a whopping 91 percent of the participants' worries did not come true. For several participants, the result was even better: none of their fears came to pass.[2]

Pause for a moment to think about the worries you have even while reading this book. Now consider those worries in the context of the research. It is likely that nine out of ten of them are not going to happen. In other words, what is putting butterflies in your stomach and causing you to bite your nails or lose sleep at night is probably nothing more than an imagination—a make-believe mind game set up to get you to settle.

Destroying the Imaginations of Fear

Did you believe in Santa Claus as a kid? I did. I believed until sometime in third grade. I was convinced that jolly ole St. Nick really slinked his way through all the chimneys in the world in a single night. As proof, I found remnants of his long, white beard caught on the branches of our Christmas tree.

When it came time for my parents to end this fairy tale, all they had to do was show me the cotton they had used to leave traces of what looked like a beard. They also needed to explain that the "Santa tracker" on the news was only a simulation. With a bit of truth—poof—Santa was gone forever.

Truth not only works to crush childhood fantasies, but it is powerful to destroy the adult fantasies, like the frightening imaginations of an unknown future. Silencing lies with truth is the spiritual principle at the heart of this book. It is a principle to which science is now awakening. That is why psychologists suggest one of the best ways to beat fear is to gather as much knowledge as possible.[3]

That is what I did before I left my job for full-time ministry. I did not simply quit my job on a whim with no research or analysis. I surveyed the opportunities and considered the confirmation of others. I also studied personal and ministry expenses in relation to the current and projected revenue. I even made some spreadsheets.

These were not, of course, my only bellwethers to know if I should step out. They were some of many indicators that I used to discern wisdom. As you will see later in this chapter, there is nothing wrong with reasonably collecting information to forecast what might be ahead. Sometimes God instructs you to do so. Opinions, numbers and spreadsheets, however, can only go so far. Since they cannot tell you what will actually happen, they cannot possibly remove all fear. That is why you still saw the doubt and trembling in my journal entry.

In truth, my practical analysis showed that my decision did not make worldly sense. The numbers did not match what any financial advisor would have said I needed to succeed. That is where God's Word dominates. When every worldly indicator warns of sure danger, God's Word contains two realities that change everything. Let's explore them now.

Fear-Silencing Reality #1: God's Presence

Moses was destined to lead God's people out of their slavery in Egypt into a land of freedom. But when God first called to him from a burning bush, Moses had every excuse as to why he could not, should not or must not be used: "Who am I to appear before Pharaoh? Who am I to lead the people of Israel out of Egypt?" (Exodus 3:11).

God's response to Moses' insecurity did not provide him with a step-by-step of what to do. It did not assure him of any material means that might help him succeed. No, God answered Moses' fear with a single promise: "I will be with you" (verse 12).

The reality of God's presence with Moses was to be the primary source of his courage and confidence. It was the foundation upon which he was to go up against the ruler of Egypt and lead God's people on a journey that began by having to walk through a sea and ended with displacing the inhabitants of a land.

The story of Israel's journey out of Egypt and into the Promised Land takes up nearly five books of the Bible (from Exodus to Joshua). An entire volume and then some could be dedicated to chronicling their forty-year trek. But at every pivotal point along the way, God's answer to fear was always His presence.

- When Moses pleaded that he was not well-spoken enough to convince Pharaoh, God insisted, "I will be with you" (Exodus 3:12).
- During their exodus while being pursued by the armies of Egypt, God said, "The LORD himself will fight for you. Just stay calm" (Exodus 14:14).
- Fifty-some days into their journey when Moses sought more help, God again guaranteed, "I will personally go with you, Moses, and I will give you rest—everything will be fine for you" (Exodus 33:14).

Do you see? At every juncture of worry along the way, God assured them that He would be with them and would fight for them.

Yet despite the promise of God's presence, He still asked them to prepare for what was ahead. To expound upon the story that we briefly explored in chapter 2, as they drew closer to the Promised Land, God spoke to Moses: "Send out men to explore the land of Canaan" (Numbers 13:2). Moses obeyed God's instructions and sent twelve men ahead to investigate the topography of the land, the quality of its soil and the strength of its inhabitants.

After forty days of collecting research and evidence, the scouts returned to the community to share their report. "It is indeed a bountiful country—a land flowing with milk and honey," they affirmed while passing around samples of its fruit (verse 27). Their joy ended there. "But the people living there are powerful, and their towns are large and fortified. We even saw giants there" (verse 28).

Upon hearing this news, the people's minds went immediately into overdrive, interpreting what this might mean. Imaginations of worst-case scenarios consumed them until the entire nation was sent into a panic from fear of certain defeat: "The land we traveled through and explored will devour anyone who goes to live there" (verse 32). Their fear was so intense, that they wished they had died.

Were there really giants living in the land? Absolutely. Were the giants physically stronger than the people of Israel? Without a doubt. If those were the only two realities by which they were to base their outcome, then they might be wise to be afraid. But there was a greater reality to consider.

It was God's presence. This is what Joshua and Caleb reminded Israel of, and it snapped them out of the spell of their feelings: "Don't be afraid of the people of the land. They are only helpless prey to us! They have no protection, but the Lord is with us! Don't be afraid of them" (Numbers 14:9).

Reawakened by truth, Israel eventually continued the journey. From time to time fears manifested, but every time God's assurance remained the same: "Be strong and courageous! Do not be afraid or discouraged. For the Lord your God is with you wherever you go" (Joshua 1:9).

Your Truth: God Is with You

I wear a ring on my right hand with God's instruction to be strong and courageous. It serves as an everyday reminder that courage is not the absence of real challenges. Being strong does not mean that I will always feel strong. But rather, despite every other piece of information that I might gather about the future, the one that matters most is that God is with me. If it is something He has called me to do or promised that I would have, nothing can get in the way of my possessing it. For not only is God with me to protect and strengthen me in the present, He goes before me to fight off the obstacles and enemies ahead. That is why when even a fearful thought enters my mind, I often cast it away with a short declaration based on this truth. I say, "God is here, even in the places that I fear."

As I said earlier, it is fine to be aware of the challenges of your journey. It is okay to be wise about your strengths and weaknesses. It is no sin to try to anticipate or mitigate some of the unknowns. Go ahead and spy out your promise. Just do not be paralyzed by the what ifs and wonderings that often come with doing so.

Keep the reality of God's presence at the top of your mind remembering that you never face today or tomorrow alone. In fact, you have it better than Moses, Joshua or Israel. God was with them, but because of Jesus, He is in you! This means that you never have to fight a battle on your own. Whatever obstacle you face does not only face you, but it faces God. And that is a losing battle for it, not you.

Fear-Silencing Reality #2: God's Faithfulness

The Christian life is undeniably a journey of trust, but God never asks us to trust Him only because He says so. God asks us to trust Him based upon what He has already done. And that is all He has ever asked of His people.

To understand what I mean, consider the experience of Adam and Eve. Freshly created as adults in a mature creation with no history to learn from, God's instructions could have been especially suspicious. They could have wondered, "Is this God really telling the truth? Should we trust him?" That is why from the get-go, before He asked anything of them, God established His character.

Immediately after God breathed His breath into Adam, the Bible recounts that He placed him in a garden where He "made all sorts of trees grow up from the ground" (Genesis 2:9). God did not just ask Adam to believe He was his Creator, but He showed him that He was. Furthermore, the Bible suggests the first couple hosted regular visits with God in the Garden. It is fun to imagine the kinds of things they might have talked about. Perhaps in that time God taught them some of what we wonder how humans learned. Things like how to grow crops, make fire and cook. Whatever the case, this time with God would have helped them get to know His heart. My point is, God did not sit in heaven and ask them to trust Him. He demonstrated His creating power and friendship, and He proved Himself to them so that they had reason to trust Him.

The same can be said about when God asked Moses to take on Pharoah and lead His people to escape the clutches of Egypt. Before God told Moses to go, He spoke to him out of the flames of a bush that did not burn up. To quench all of Moses' what ifs, God performed signs in front of his eyes. The story of the exodus of Israel's people from Egypt to the Promised Land is filled with more demonstrations of God's character than I have the space here to retell. Two of the highlights are creating a dry path through the Red Sea for the people to escape and miraculously providing food every morning of their journey. While the voyage to their promise included wild leaps of faith and risks unrivaled by anything you or I have ever had to do, they were given plenty of reason to trust that the God who promised to be with them would be faithful to provide and protect.

Still, as we have seen in their story, the propensity of people to discount God's presence because of what they see, hear or feel in the moment is strong. That is why God asked them to frequently retell the stories of His power and to establish physical reminders of His goodness. Upon entering the Promised Land, the Lord instructed that a memorial be built (see Joshua 4:1–7). He also told His people to annually celebrate Passover to remember the miracle of their deliverance from Egypt. God knew that reflecting upon His goodness in the past was the key to courage in the future.

Years later, Israel's future king David used this principle to take down a giant named Goliath. At the time, David was young and inexperienced in battle. Goliath, on the other hand, had been a man of war from his youth and was considered a champion for the Philistines. Everyone knew that David was no match for this giant. I am sure David feared it, too.

Despite the stark difference in stature and experience, David boldly took on this gnarly beast of a man with the confidence he developed by reflecting on God's faithfulness in his history. David suited up courageously for the conflict boasting, "The LORD who rescued me from the claws of the lion and the bear will rescue me from this Philistine" (1 Samuel 17:37). David's courage to confront Goliath was not founded upon his own ability to achieve a victory but on God's, because he had experienced God do it before.

Your Truth: You Are Still Here

My history with God is what gives me the faith to make bold moves. Leaving my job for full-time ministry was the biggest risk I had taken up to that point. I did not know where the money would come from. I was not sure I would have enough to say. But by the time God called me to take this step, I had learned that I didn't need to be sure. God had always provided. Any time that I heard, "You should be afraid," I silenced that voice by reflecting on moments I had feared I would never make it through, but I had. It did not always take away the nervousness, but it instilled the courage in me to push through knowing that somehow, someway, God would make a way again. And He did.

You also have a history with God. The proof is that you are still here! You are reading these words, which means that you made it through challenges you never thought you would: tests you dreaded you would never pass, bills you were certain would never go away or symptoms you feared would be the end of you. Sure, maybe not everything worked out as you wished. Undoubtedly, there has been pain and grief along the way. That is life. But in one way or another, God brought you right here to this moment.

Think about this: you have a 100 percent survival rate through everything you have been through so far. There is no reason to believe that will change today.

Getting beyond Your Fears

John Wesley is perhaps one of the greatest known theologians and evangelists in Christian history. Throughout his ministry in the 1700s, he fervently opposed the slave trade, supported women in ministry, ignited a revolution within the Church of England and founded the Methodist church. In his day, these were bold stances and big risks, all of which brought him sharp criticism and persecution.

With such a record, admirers looked to Wesley as a model of courage. Perhaps that is why one man pulled him aside for advice on how to overcome fear.

"I do not know what I shall do with all this worry and trouble," the man confided. While on their walk, Wesley noticed a cow looking over a stone wall.

Then with sudden wit that seemed like divine inspiration, he asked, "Do you know why that cow is looking over the wall?"

"No," said the man.

"The cow is looking over the wall because she cannot see through it," Wesley observed. "That is what you must do with your wall of trouble—look over it."[4]

What obstacle stares you in the face that provokes feelings of fear? What challenge holds you back from pursuing a promise or simply enjoying your life? If you stay fixated on it, you will never get beyond it. If you wait for it to go away, you will never progress. Take the advice of Wesley and look over it. Every time the whisper, "You should be afraid," pushes itself into your mind with all its imaginations and speculations, push it out with the truth that God is with you, He goes before you and He will never leave you. Call to mind the record of your history with Him. Through everything you have ever feared, He has brought you through, and you are still here. The challenges you see now will likely be cleared out by the time you arrive. And if they are not, God's grace will get you through when you get there—as it always has.

Now that we have confronted the feeling of fear, let's get more specific and confront one of the most common and most paralyzing voices of fear: "You don't belong." Join me to shut up this lie in the next chapter.

Speak It!

God is with me and before me; therefore, I have all the strength, provision and protection I need to get through what is here and what is ahead. Just as He has delivered me in the past, I know He will be faithful to do it again. I have nothing to fear!

Questions for Personal Reflection

1. What is your most common reaction to fear? Why do you think you react this way?

2. What fears do you face about your present or future? Take some time to write them out, then separate the realities from the interpretations.

3. Using the list of fears that you just created, apply the truths that God is with you and before you to the realities. How does this change your interpretation of what could happen?

4. Our testimonies of the past are powerful building blocks for our future. What events in your history with God can you use to develop courage for the future?

5. What is one small step you can take today that would ignore the voice of fear and display strength and courage?

10

"You do not belong."

We have all been there—peering in from the outside of some group we desperately want to be part of. Maybe it is a place on the sports team, a spot in the sorority or the inner circle of influencers at work or at church. Yet getting in seems, well, impossible for someone like you, because

"You are not athletic enough."
"You are not attractive enough."
"You are not smart enough."
"You are too quiet."
"You are too passionate."
"You are too awkward."

Voices that insist that "You are too much of this," or "You are too little of that," make you believe you could never be wanted. "You are worthless," they contend. "You don't belong."

It is human nature to crave acceptance. Psychologists consider the sense of belonging a fundamental need alongside air, water, food and safety.[1] That is hardly a breakthrough discovery, though. Humans have been wired for relationship from the beginning.

Just after Adam was created, God determined that he needed something more. Not another plant or animal. He needed something to which he could relate. Man needed someone who could speak his language and understand his experiences. That is why God declared, "It is not good for the man to be alone" (Genesis 2:18). Adam needed another human. So God created Eve.

The pursuit of acceptance is not evil; it is natural. The problem is that most of us go about it in all the wrong ways. We end up chasing a false sense of acceptance that never satisfies but instead breeds insecurity and inadequacy in us.

Fitting In versus Belonging

In the creation story, Adam was first formed, defined and named by God. The companion God brought was suited for how he was made.

Don't we pursue relationships backward from that? We find a group or a person with whom we want to belong and then seek to fit in. But fitting in is that—it is fitting. It is shaping. It is changing or giving up something of yourself to match something else.

In the process of trying to fit in, you lose who God created you to be. You become nothing more than a mirror of those from whom you seek acceptance, so that when they look at you, they see themselves and not you.[2] The hope is that they will like what they see. But if they do, then you have a bigger problem. Because what you attract them with is what you must keep them with. And that is anything but freedom.

My friend Angie was once a perfect example of the slavery of fitting in and where it leads. In school, she was not an outcast. She was the one who enjoyed a seat at the popular kids' lunch table. Her bubbly cheerleader personality made it easy for her to be liked, so much so that she was voted homecoming queen her senior year.

But popularity came with great expectations. Some expectations were given by others, and some were self-imposed. "Among my peers, I couldn't be the nerdy Star Wars enthusiast I really was," she recalled. "I had labels to live up to and an impossible social status to maintain." So she did what she believed was necessary to keep the acceptance of her peers: lots of drugs and alcohol. "It was sad," Angie admitted. "For too many years, I pretended to be something I was not out of the fear I wouldn't be accepted for how God created me."

Being accepted for how God created you is the benchmark of real belonging. That is what you should pursue. To be sure, it might not bring you popularity from the masses. Your authentic self probably will not suit everyone's fancies. To experience belonging, often your social circle must shrink before it ever has a chance to expand. When that happens, do not believe the lie that something is wrong with you. Social pruning is a good thing. Embrace it. It is an opportunity to be who you are meant to be and to do what you are meant to do with the people with whom you are meant to do it.

This is exactly what the enemy does not want. Your God-given identity is your greatest threat to him. That is why, as we have already explored in this book, he works in very deceptive ways to get you to give it up. Capitalizing on your need for belonging is another one of those ways. But hear me, God did not make you as you are so that you would hide who you are. No, He deliberately made you—with all your quirks and qualities—for a beautiful and powerful purpose.

Now, let's consider the two foundations of your worth and why you belong.

Foundation #1: You Are Handpicked by God

The apostle Paul's protégé, Timothy, was born a "mistake" within his culture. His mother was Jewish while his father was Greek. This intermingling of race was a big no-no according to Jewish law.

In our modern perspective, it is hard to comprehend what the issue is. But back then, a boy from a mixed union faced enormous consequences that would have left him excluded from his peers. He could not have been educated with other Jewish boys, marry a Jewish woman or participate in any of the Jewish festivals, all because of something he did not choose. For those reasons, society labeled Timothy as being wrong, and it rejected him.

But society was wrong. Despite the circumstances of his birth, Paul selected him as his missionary partner to help build God's Church. Tradition says he became the bishop of the church at Ephesus. The world might not have wanted him, but God did.

Do you battle feeling as if you are a mistake because of something you did not choose for yourself? Maybe even because of the way you were born? I am the youngest of four boys by a lot. My closest brother is eight years older than me. I know you are probably thinking that I was an accident. Believe me, I have thought that, too.

My parents, however, swear that is not the case. I am not sure I believe them, but over time, I have realized that it does not matter. The fact is, I am here. And so are you. How, when and the condition in which you entered this world have no bearing on your worth because the Bible assures God chose you long before you were born (see Ephesians 1:4).

As I said a few chapters ago, you are no surprise to God. You did not emerge from the womb and leave God scrambling to figure out what to do with you. Your birth did not put heaven in a crisis. God knew what He was getting before you were news to your parents, and He brought you into existence anyway. If you are the product of some oops or accident, think of it this way: God wanted you in this world so badly that He used an unconventional or unexpected way to do it!

Be encouraged that God does not make decisions in the same way humans do. The Bible makes that evident. As He was choosing David to be king, God revealed, "People judge by outward appearance, but the LORD looks at the heart" (1 Samuel 16:7).

God's choice is not based upon family history. He chose Abraham from a family of idol worshipers to be the father of the faith. His choice is not based upon an impeccable past. He chose Rahab, a former prostitute, to fill an important spot in Jesus' lineage. God's choice is not about strength. He chose Gideon, the self-proclaimed weakest man in his tribe, to be the deliverer of Israel. As we explored with Timothy, His choice is not based on the right circumstances. God does not choose based upon gender, either. In a day when the testimony of a woman was not trusted, God chose Mary

Magdalene as the first person to announce the resurrection of Jesus.

And God chose you, too! Yes, you! You with the past of pain and promiscuity. You who felt as if your parents never really wanted you. You who struggle with disabilities and differences that make you question if you belong, that make you feel as if you are wrong. You who have been told all your life that you do not have what it takes to succeed. God chose you.

Foundation #2: You Are Handcrafted by God

Regardless of the circumstances of how you came to be, one thing that is certain is that you are made in God's image. Remember that this is at the foundation of why God loves you unconditionally. It is also what makes you more valuable than everything else in creation, and it is more evidence of why you belong.

After creation's conception, God spoke to His newly birthed earth to bring about every kind of plant and animal: "Let the land sprout with vegetation. . . . Let the earth produce every sort of animal" (Genesis 1:11, 24).

Next, God did something very different. Rather than speak to the land to produce, God spoke to Himself to add something of His own semblance: "Let us make human beings in our image, to be like us" (verse 26). To do this, God used more than His mouth to create; He personally formed Adam and Eve with His own hands. The Bible summarizes His crowning achievement: "So God created human beings in his own image. In the image of God he created them" (verse 27).

The contrast between the creation of plants and animals and the creation of people is stark. So that you do not miss the significance, allow me to highlight it once more. Everything seen inside of creation reflects creation, and it is brought forth from the land by a command from God's mouth. No doubt, that is powerful! But only humankind reflects God Himself. We were brought forth by His personal touch.

The truth that every person is created in God's image is a staggering notion. It is all the more extraordinary when you consider what an image is meant to do. By definition, an image is a representation or a reflection of something. Simply put, God created people to reflect and demonstrate facets of who He is. Nothing else in creation can do that. Only you and I can.

So many of us resent our differences, believing they are what count us out or deem us unacceptable. We spend oodles of time, energy and money working to look like everyone else—to be "normal." But what if our differences are by design? What if they each reflect a unique aspect of God that He wants on display? Maybe that is the real battle. Maybe we are striving desperately to hide what God wants seen!

Consider these following ways that you might uniquely reflect God.

Your body is a reflection of God.

We all have at least one thing that we believe is a glaring physical imperfection. It is something we think everyone notices the moment they see us. You might even have more than one thing. Off the top of my head, I could rattle off at least a dozen things that I have wished were different about my physical appearance. A few extra inches of height would be nice. Thicker bones would be nice, too. For years, I hated how pale my skin was. And I have never been fond of the shape of my nose or my eyes. It is so easy to get carried away with this!

Why do we passionately dislike certain physical features about ourselves? I suspect it is because we are inundated with media that casts a model of perfection. It is a model that none of us—not even the models themselves—can achieve without a slew of computer touch-ups.

You will never find a place in Scripture where God asks people to wish for different features. He never calls a natural-born quality about someone unattractive or unwanted. Instead, the Bible reasons that every quality is a reflection of our Creator:

> You made all the delicate, inner parts of my body and knit me together in my mother's womb. Thank you for making me so wonderfully complex! Your workmanship is marvelous— how well I know it.
>
> Psalm 139:13–14

David acknowledged that his physical features were not the product of happenstance, but of God's choosing. He goes on to describe being "woven together in the dark of the womb" (verse 15).

You and I were made the same way. Jesus revealed that God numbered the hairs on your head (see Luke 12:7). The shape of your nose and teeth, your height, your bone structure and the color of your hair and eyes—none of these are unaccounted for. Each variety stems from God's image.

Skin color may be the best example of the vast degrees of difference that can come from one source. Scholars believe that Adam and Eve were created with medium brown skin. This not only fits with the region of the world in which they lived, but it is in line with the variations of skin color today. You can research the science behind this, but in short, medium brown contains all the genetic information necessary to produce every color of skin, from the whitest of white to the blackest of black. Hair color, eye color and the shapes of your features work similarly.[3] Not one is better than another. Not one is godlier. We are all one race with physical differences that come from the God we reflect (see Acts 17:26).

Your personality and passions are a reflection of God.

For years, I despised my introverted personality. I was sure it was given to me by the devil to stand in the way of what God had called me to do. So I tried to change it through prayer, exercises and deliverance. But despite my best efforts, my personality did not go anywhere. That is when I sensed God telling me to settle down. *I gave you that personality,* I felt Him assure.

Since then, I have come to celebrate my nature. I have realized that I can do things as an introvert that others cannot. In fact, that part of me is what makes me successful at my work. Sure, I might not be the life of the party or a comedian preacher, but the energy I derive from alone time makes me introspective and motivated to mine for deep insights. These are qualities that come out in my writing and teaching.

Extroverts, of course, can do things that I cannot. I often envy the leadership skills, networking ability and sheer knack that some of my extroverted friends have for working a room of strangers. I hate small talk. But I am grateful that some people love it!

None of us have everything. We each have a part, which is why God created us to all work together as a Body. Personality

159

types belong and have their place because they are reflections of God's image.

So are your skills and passions. Freshly made in God's image, Adam was tasked to tend and watch over the Garden of Eden (see Genesis 2:15). His job was not only to grow food, but to protect and develop the beauty of the garden.

Just as God gave Adam the ability to do this job, He later gave others very different abilities for very different reasons. On Israel's way to the Promised Land, God asked His people to construct a place that would host His presence and where they could make offerings during the journey. To help build it all, God gifted people with a variety of skills and passions: "I have given special skill to all the gifted craftsmen so they can make all the things I have commanded" (Exodus 31:6). What the people constructed was not any ole place. God gifted different people with different skills to build a beautiful place that was filled with ornate engravings, gemstones, gold and silver.

What are you passionate about? What talents do you have? Have you considered that your interests might be God-given and not coincidental? I am not only referring to ministry gifts, but to the talents of the teacher, the doctor, the scientist, the artist, the entertainer, the stay-at-home parent, and yes, even the politician. The skills and passions that empower every vocation (as long as they are not something sinful, of course) are given sacredly by God to help cultivate His world with beauty and sophistication.

I have heard it said that it is no accident that the Bible begins in a garden but ends in a city. Your gifts are a large part of God's plan to get there. You were handcrafted to express and create in a unique way that comes directly from God.

Your situation is a reflection of God.

If I may challenge you a bit further, perhaps your situation or the stage of your life is a reflection of God. Hear me out. I am not referring to some sort of unfortunate circumstance such as a disaster, disease or trauma. We have established already that these kinds of events are not from the hand of God. But I am talking about the places or positions in which you currently find yourself, some of which you may detest.

Let's contrast singleness and marriage, for example. Many single people despise their "condition" and are desperate to find someone. That is natural. As I said earlier, the pursuit of relationship is wired into us. Still, I know far too many married people who, after the newness wears off, crave the freedom of their single friends. As it is often said, the grass is greener on the other side. It is human nature, it seems, to want what you do not have.

Singles are often quick to complain that the modern Church elevates marriage over singleness. I have found that is because many of today's ministers mistake God's declaration, "It is not good for the man to be alone" to mean marriage (Genesis 2:18). Yet single does not mean alone. God's declaration is a statement of belonging that can also be found in friends, family and other close communities.

Having said this, both marriage and singleness are powerful and necessary expressions of God. Marriage is God's earthly representation of the eternal union between Christ and His Church. That is beautiful. Singleness, on the other hand, is God's demonstration of the sufficiency of Christ in His heavenly Kingdom where there is no human marriage. That is also beautiful. Neither situation is better, more God-honoring or more complete than the other. Each reflects an aspect of who God is that both the Church and the world desperately need to see today.

I am only musing here, but perhaps the different Christian denominations, which many regard as divisive, reflect distinct characteristics of God's image. Is it possible that the fundamentalists and their emphasis on God's Word, the charismatics and their emphasis on God's presence, the liturgists and their emphasis on reverence, and the "gracists" and their emphasis on love and compassion, each reflect something that God wants to convey about Himself? Too often we treat each other as enemies when all these expressions are found in Christ. Do they not all somehow belong?

"For all who will ever believe in me," Jesus prayed to His Father, "may they be one, just as you and I are one" (see John 17:20–21). To this end, I do not expect that the denominations will suddenly take up each other's causes or celebrate each other's distinct doctrines. The Church is called the body of Christ precisely because it is made of many different parts, each serving a unique role and purpose. No single part can do everything nor help everyone. But perhaps the unity Jesus prayed for could be realized by respecting each other's place, message and situation as a piece of God's heart, even with a bit of healthy tension.

Remember, the goal of Christianity is not to become a spouse, parent, minister, philanthropist or missionary. Beyond consensus about the life, death and resurrection of Christ, it is not to conform to a certain way of thinking or political affiliation. The goal of Christianity is not to become anything except more and more like Jesus. And in Him, there is a place for a wide variety of looks, personalities, passions, skills and situations.

You Are God's Masterpiece

You were handpicked and handcrafted as a beautiful reflection of your Creator. Do you know what you call something like that? A masterpiece. That is what God calls it, too: "For we are God's masterpiece. He has created us anew in Christ Jesus, so we can do the good things he planned for us long ago" (Ephesians 2:10).

We all know what a masterpiece is. It is a creator's prized piece, his or her most valuable work. Artists are blessed if they have a single masterpiece. Few throughout history are fortunate enough to have had more. Beethoven is one of them. So is Vincent van Gogh. So is Michelangelo.

Though each represent different kinds of art, they all share a common feature of their repeated success. Beethoven, who was totally deaf, composed his symphonies in a void of sound. Born with a brain lesion, Van Gogh battled mania and depression. He had to find vision in the midst of chaos and emptiness. Michelangelo famously credits his sculptures to a single principle: "I saw the angel in the marble and carved until I set him free."[4] Do you see? Some of the greatest masterpieces by the greatest artists are created out of something that nobody else could recognize.

No artist, of course, compares to God. Imagine the most beautiful sights you have ever seen in creation. Maybe the snowcapped mountains, the northern lights, a field of brilliantly colored wildflowers or waves crashing into a towering cliff. Out of nothing, God brought forth these masterpieces. He saw them for what they were long before anyone else could.

That is how God sees you. I know that right now your life might not look like anything of value to others or to yourself, but the truths we explored all throughout this chapter affirm that long ago God saw the value in you, because He placed it there! That is why He chose to bring you into existence. Today you may be surrounded by obstacles, and your greatest features might be hidden under layers of insecurity, fear, struggle or shame. Even as you read, God is working to remove those layers. Just know that there is a masterpiece in you that you do not have to prove, you just have to reveal. When you do, the right people will recognize it.

God chose and molded you—but not to fit a mold. The thing about a masterpiece is that it is made to stand out. As many masterpieces as Beethoven, Van Gogh and Michelangelo created, not a single one was the same. They each were wildly unique and were crafted to express a unique part of their creator's heart.

As are you!

Friend, you are no mistake, nor the product of some random chance. You are the outcome of God's choosing, the result of His steady hand. Yes, you belong as you are with all your quirks and qualities because with them, not despite them, you reflect something about God that the world needs to see.

While all of this is incredible and encouraging, you should be aware that the enemy will try to convince you that you need to be like somebody else to succeed. I am sure you have heard that before. Building on everything you have learned, let's take down this lie next.

Speak It!

I am handpicked and handcrafted by God to reflect Him in a unique way. My looks, personality, passions and situations do not count me out—they count me in. Yes, I am God's masterpiece, and I belong on display just as He made me!

Questions for Personal Reflection

1. What about you or your experiences has led you to believe that you cannot be accepted by others? Why does that "thing" seem unacceptable?

2. Was there a time in the past when you gave up something of yourself in order to be accepted? What was the result of that?

3. Was there a time in the past when you revealed the real you? How did people respond? How did that feel?

4. What aspects of your body, personality, passions and situation reflect God's image and represent His heart? What might God want to use them to demonstrate?

5. How does the truth that you are handpicked and handcrafted by God shift how you will respond to God and people in the future?

11

"You need to be like somebody else."

With today's media, do you feel the ever-present temptation to compare yourself to someone else? Do you often envy someone else's success? Are you tempted to duplicate what they do, thinking that it will achieve the same for you? It is a strange but common deception to believe that being someone else will help you find yourself.

I have been caught up in this, too. Sadly, as a young minister who has been discovering my voice and message, I have too often examined other preachers as case studies. There was a season during which I could hardly attend a conference, watch a message or read a book without sizing myself up against the speaker or author. In these moments, I would get absolutely nothing out of the message because I was too focused on studying their style or format or trying to figure out the secret sauce of their success. Resultantly, my "I need to do" and "I need to be" lists grew fairly large with things, such as,

"I need to tell more stories."
"I need to be more humorous."
"I need signs and wonders."
"I need to wear skinnier jeans!"

I could not, of course, possibly incorporate all the success traits I saw in other preachers that I believed I lacked. At least, not without looking like a circus act.

One day, God's voice broke mercifully through all the others. *Why don't you just be you? You have a unique personality, style and story that can reach people others can't. Use the gift of you.*

Me—a gift? I had never really thought of myself in those terms. I focused mostly outward, wondering why others had what I desired—an opportunity, a better personality, a house, a spouse or a bank account. I never looked inward to consider what I had that others did not. God's encouragement challenged me to consider what package of traits I have that enable me to do something unique.

Have you ever thought that who you are is a gift? Sure, not everything about you is wonderful. Like anyone, you have aspects of your innate nature and personality that need some smoothing out. The Holy Spirit will work with you on those areas. But if you remember from the last chapter, we are made in God's image. We each reflect aspects of His personality, character and heart. I might be introverted, serious, structured, ministry-minded and a bit geeky. You might be extroverted, jovial, free-spirited, music-minded and a hipster. Someone else might be a mix of the two of us but also athletic.

Obviously, there is a myriad of personality types, giftings, interests and situations beyond what I mentioned that make up who someone is. No two people share the exact same combination. Like a fingerprint, you have been gifted with your distinctions in order that you can make a unique imprint.

Even the things that are quirky about you—maybe *especially* those things—are what really set you apart for a purpose. Think about some of your favorite Bible heroes. Many who are the most memorable are also the ones who were extra peculiar. Consider the prophet Jeremiah. His personality was sensitive, serious, introspective and shy. He also remained single. His traits sometimes caused him to be rejected by others. Occasionally, they caused him to reject himself.

I am sure that Jeremiah lamented, "Why can't I be more like somebody else?" But he was handcrafted by God to be a last attempt to turn Israel's heart back to Him. Jeremiah's unique traits were suited perfectly to reach a people who had abandoned God because of a mistaken belief that God had abandoned them. After all, who better to assure God's nearness and faithfulness than someone who could literally say, "I sat alone because [God's] hand was on me" (Jeremiah 15:17)?

And then there is the apostle Paul. Raised as a Pharisee, he was dogmatic and zealous by nature, so much so that he was once the leading persecutor of Christians who pillaged the early Church—until he met Jesus. But even his miraculous encounter with Christ did not change his personality.

169

And for good reason, I would say. His over-the-top temperament coupled with his dramatic story of persecutor-turned-apostle gave him the drive and attention he needed to succeed in God's plan to spread the faith.

Jeremiah and Paul are but two of many Bible heroes whose success in their calling came particularly because of their particulars. They were different because they were designed to be. And so are you. Yes, there is a reason God made you for such a time as this, and it is definitely not because you are like everyone else!

The Secret behind Social Media

Depression is a complicated battle, and I will not lump it into a single cause. But psychologists claim that one significant reason why it affects more people than ever is because we are inundated with media that portrays other's lives as being perfect while we are living in the behind-the-scenes of our own very imperfect lives.[1]

Get this—today, the average American spends about ten hours per day behind a screen.[2] Not surprisingly, much of that time is spent scrolling through perhaps the greatest purveyor of dissatisfaction, discouragement and depression—social media.

You know the drill. You are bored while waiting—waiting at a stop light, waiting for your food to arrive, waiting for the workday or school day to end or waiting to become tired enough to fall sleep. So you reach for your phone. Without needing to look at your phone, the muscle-memory of your fingers moves them right to your favorite social app. Suddenly, you have escaped the mundane that is your real life, and you have entered fantasy land. Really.

As you swipe mindlessly through post after post and photo after photo, you grow increasingly insecure. That is because you are confronted with the highlights of everyone else. Steve became vice president of his company. Katie and Chris posed in front of their brand-new three-story home. Your high school friend shared a selfie with her picture-perfect family on vacation in Hawaii. Another friend lost fifty pounds on some multilevel-marketing ice cream diet.

As you scroll, an ugly emotion rises within you. You are not happy for any of them! You live in a two-bedroom apartment. You are not even in middle management, much less executive leadership. You have been told you cannot have children. And too much ice cream is the reason you do not look as you did in high school! In only a few swipes, their success makes you question your entire existence. Suddenly, you feel inadequate, like a failure and worthless. Cue the depression.

I will let you in on a secret. Behind the screens of their social profiles, the lives of your near or distant friends are not as fantastic as you think. They may even post their highlights as a way to compensate for the same insecurity you face. That is how this vicious cycle perpetuates.

Some years ago, I saw the reality of this played out on my Facebook page. I was in North Carolina for a weekend speaking engagement. Part of the event included a men's golf tournament that the pastor invited me to join. Now, please understand, though I played some golf in my youth, mostly for a golf merit badge in Boy Scouts, I definitely would not call myself a golfer.

Oh, but I took a photo that looked as if I was! I wore a souvenir hat from a golf course I had visited (but not played at) a decade earlier. My crisply pressed polo shirt was tucked into white chino pants. I sported the golf shoes and gloves.

Looking all pro while posed on the green, I snapped a selfie and sent it to my feed.

Within minutes, dozens of comments flooded in. "I didn't know you golf!" someone exclaimed. "When can we go together?" another asked. My favorite, "Looks like you're living the dream!"

The dream? I laughed to myself. It was more like a nightmare! Those eighteen holes I played were more of a lesson in humility and withstanding embarrassment than anything else! The photo captured a few-seconds highlight of the day. What it did not show were the dozens of swings and misses, the lost balls and the nowhere-near-the-hole putts.

That photo was anything but reality. But to the masses on social media, it completely looked as if it were reality. Unfortunately, I am sure many compared their lives to what they thought mine was. Even more sadly, I am sure some experienced insecurity and discouragement about their own lives because of it.

The Ugly Root of Envy

With this kind of influence, it is no wonder one of the first suggestions counselors make when someone complains of depression is to have their clients take a break from social media.[3] Time away from fantasyland can do wonders to recalibrate yourself to what is real and what really matters. But for those who for whatever reason cannot get away from it, there is also that fun little unfollow button. You know, the one that hides a person's posts but allows you to stay friends with them. I have tapped that button at least a time or two.

One time, I tapped it because a wicked sense of jealousy came over me when I saw an old friend's posts. In the span of a few days, he shared what seemed like dozens of photos of himself in some new opportunity, almost as if he was trying to prove something. This struck a deep nerve of insecurity in me. So I clicked unfollow.

Whatever the motivation he had for his insistent posts, they were no excuse for my reaction. That is why as soon as I tapped the button, I heard, *Better than unfollowing him would be for you to become satisfied with your own life.*

Ouch! That was hard to hear, but it was true. My battle with envy had nothing to do with social media or the specific situation that was making me envious. And while taking a break from the platforms or unfollowing someone undoubtedly has benefits, in my case, doing so would have only masked the symptoms of a deeper root that existed in me on or off the internet.

I suspect that is the case for most people. Jealousy can arise at school, work or in the family. That is why you must get at the root of not being satisfied with your life when you are dealing with comparison and all its ugly symptoms. The cure is to find success in the unique gifts and plan God has for you. Let's continue on to see how.

Redefining Your Success

Words change with time. The word *success* is one that is currently in the midst of an evolution. Consider Webster's definition in 1828. It defined *success* as "the favorable or prosperous termination of any thing attempted."[4] That is pretty straightforward. Today, however, another definition has crept in that is quickly taking precedence. Today the definition includes "getting or achieving wealth, respect or fame."[5]

To have *success* be defined as termination of things attempted means that achieving it is different for different people. But because of what we just discussed, achieving wealth, respect and fame are quickly becoming the new measuring stick of success. In that definition, there is no room for uniqueness of calling. Success is hinged entirely on being rich or popular. It is no wonder people prop up their lives on social media to project fame and fortune. It is also no wonder people intensely battle insecurity, inadequacy and dissatisfaction.

Real satisfaction for your life comes from getting your definition of success in sync with God's. And His definition is not often what seems right in the eyes of the world. It is not what somebody else is doing. It is not the amount of money in the bank, all the ladders climbed, having the trophy wife or the number of likes. No, real success is much simpler and more fulfilling. It is obedience to God's plan.

Israel's first king, Saul, learned a hard lesson about obedience that caused him to forfeit his throne. During a conquest of Israel's enemies, God instructed Saul to destroy all the defeated nation's assets. But Saul was not entirely obedient. He only destroyed what he deemed was worthless or of poor quality. He kept the best of the spoils—the sheep, goats and cattle—for himself (see 1 Samuel 15:9).

In the eyes of the world, this made good sense. It was customary to keep the plunder when overtaking another nation. Saul even appears proud of himself for doing it with good intentions. When confronted by the prophet Samuel about his decision he insisted, "It's true that the army spared the best. . . . But they are going to sacrifice them to the Lord" (verse 15).

Samuel's response silenced the pride Saul had about all he gathered. "What is more pleasing to the Lord: your burnt offerings and sacrifices or your obedience to his voice?" (verse 22). This was a rhetorical question that Samuel matter-of-factly answered in his next breath. "Listen! Obedience is better than sacrifice, and submission is better than offering the fat of rams" (verse 22).

Samuel's question to Saul is one we need to ask ourselves. What is more important? All the assets you can collect? All the numbers you can achieve for God, such as the people in the seats, books sold or offerings given? Or doing what God has asked of you, even if it does not appear as sensible or impressive to the world?

I know that for ministers there is a pervasive notion that their success is based on the size of their church or the numbers of the crowd they can draw at a conference. No doubt, some people are called to lead large churches and speak to thousands at a time. But not everyone. We need churches and meetings of every size because there are people of every kind. Not everyone is comfortable attending a megachurch. Some people need specialized instruction on specific topics that will not appeal to the masses. Success might be faithfully pastoring a small church or hosting events of dozens, not thousands.

For those in the marketplace, perhaps God has called them to climb the corporate ladder of influence. But maybe He has called them to be a consistent and faithful influence for Christ to their co-workers. For parents, success might not be about something that they do, but someone they raise. For you, success might not be about the money you made but the memories you made.

Do not hold to a definition of success that is not meant to define you. What is God asking of you? If you are being obedient to that, then you are a success.

Complementing Not Competing

Around 27 years old, I was in my last year of seminary and bubbling with passion to make some kind of a difference. I had not yet discerned the message God would give me, but I knew I wanted to inspire people with hope. So using a film studio that my employer generously provided, I hosted interviews with people who had dramatic stories of God's power.

Because I was frequently accompanied by people who had supernatural experiences or giftings, others assumed I ministered similarly. By this I mean prophetically or with an emphasis on signs and wonders. To be sure, I celebrate those gifts, and I value the power of God that flows through some people for healing and deliverance.

In time, my newfound exposure brought opportunities to speak in churches. As exciting as this was, I felt the pressure to operate as those with whom I associated. The problem was that this never felt natural for me. Do not get me wrong. I am passionate and enthusiastic when I speak, but I am a teacher. I often felt as if my hosts wanted a supernatural experience and not a teacher.

Whether my sense was real or self-made didn't matter. The fear that I might not meet an expectation created some of the traps of comparison I mentioned at the beginning of this chapter. When I tried to incorporate other styles of ministry, I was only left frustrated. I would default inevitably back to, well, me. Consequently, I questioned my calling. "Am I really gifted for ministry?" I begged God to know.

His answer was gentle but direct. *Yes, Kyle, there are things others can do better than you, but there are also things you can do better than them. It is not that one gift is better than the other. They are all necessary in the Body of Christ.* He went on to confirm my gifting in a way I had not considered. *You are a healer, but you heal with words.*

For too long, I essentially apologized for being me. "I'm just a teacher," I would answer sheepishly to anyone who asked about my role in ministry. After God's assurance, I dropped the *just*. There is no hiding my gift, nor is there a need to. It is evident throughout everything I do, including this book. My style is to lay out a premise and guide people to a conclusion specifically about who God is and who we are to Him. Teaching is how God accomplishes His healing through me. And it is what brings me the most satisfaction.

How God comforted me is ultimately how the apostle Paul encouraged the church of Rome. Evidently, they also compared themselves to each other, determining who was most important according to the level of their gifts. To squelch the comparison, Paul described God's people as a Body that has many parts, each of which has a special function: "In his grace, God has given us different gifts for doing certain things well" (Romans 12:6). Paul went on to detail some of these gifts that include prophesy, serving, teaching, encouraging, giving, leadership and kindness.

This is not a complete catalog of every possible gift a Christian can have. As we saw in the last chapter, some gifts include trade skills, others are ministry roles and still others are gifts of supernatural power that come with the Holy Spirit. Though you might have several of them, there is usually one that is dominant. But nobody has them all.

While God is the one who is responsible for gracing you with your gifts, you are responsible for stewarding them. That is why Paul exhorts, "If your gift is serving others, serve them well. If you are a teacher, teach well" (verse 7). And so on. This is why knowing and embracing your unique identity in Christ is so important. When you know who you are, you know what to do. And you are most satisfied when you are doing it.

Think about it this way. If I know I am a mind or a mouth in the Body, then I will do what a mind or mouth does, which is to think or speak. I will be happy doing it. You might be a heart, hand or foot. Each of those has distinct but equally important roles. But if a hand envies a mouth and then attempts to duplicate what it does, it will strive and strive and never be satisfied. That is not because the hand is anything less. It was designed for something else—to point, show, serve, write, create, color, steer, conduct, lift or gift. Likewise, while a mouth can make great speeches, inspire and instruct, it will always fail if it attempts to pick something up—no matter how hard it tries.

I must reemphasize what Paul said. We are given different gifts for doing certain things well. We were not given the same gifts for doing everything well. As God encouraged me, He also encourages you. Yes, other people can do certain things better than you, but you can do certain things better than them. What are your talents? What do you enjoy? What energizes you? Capitalize on and develop whatever one or two top traits you have. Do not wish for someone else's gifts. His or her grace will not work for you. In the Body of Christ, we each succeed when we complement each other, not compete to be each other.

You Are Uniquely Equipped

The giant Goliath had challenged God's people to a fight they could not avoid (see 1 Samuel 17). Goliath stood between Israel and the land they were promised. Their freedom hinged upon taking down this Philistine monster.

As we explored in chapter 9, David shocked his people when he insisted that he be the one to fight. Since he was young and inexperienced in battle, he had some convincing to do. Undeniably, there were other men more proven and better equipped for the challenge.

With a bit of persuading, King Saul finally consented— but with a caveat. He requested that David go to battle in his armor, fully equipped with a bronze helmet, breastplate and sword. Since these tools were what helped bring Saul success in his assignments, he figured that they would work for David, too.

But they did not. Saul's equipment felt strange to David. "I can't go in these," he protested. "I'm not used to them." He proceeded to strip himself of what was not his and pick up only what was: five smooth stones, his shepherd's bag, his staff and his sling (see 1 Samuel 17:39–40).

Outfitted in what seemed like so little, nobody predicted David's success. Certainly, Goliath considered him no threat. "Am I a dog, that you come at me with a stick?" he taunted (see verse 43). But David did not need all the military might that others needed. He knew that it was God's plan for him to defeat Goliath. He knew the only way to succeed in this plan was to do it with what God had equipped him. And he did succeed. Much to the amazement of everyone, what David brought to the battle was enough to bring the giant down.

There is a profound lesson in this story. While others seemed better equipped and more experienced, David was the one who was called. And as God does, He does not call someone to achieve His plan using the gifts or style of someone else. No, God uniquely equips people with what they need to succeed for the way He wants them to do it.

Likewise, you are equipped with your personality, style, story and skills for a purpose that others cannot fulfill. Be assured, the world does not need an imitation of someone else. The world needs you to be uniquely you.

Naturally, this begs the question, What is the purpose that only you can fulfill? Maybe you have heard that you do not have a purpose. That is a lie! You most certainly have a purpose. It may be different than you think, but it is also nearer and easier to fulfill than you think. I will show you in the next chapter.

Speak It!

I do not need to be like anybody else. God has given me a personality, style, story and skills to fulfill something nobody else can. I am a success according to the custom design, gifts and plan He has for me.

Questions for Personal Reflection

1. What is your custom, God-given combination of personality, style, story and skills? In your notes app or on a piece of paper, write this out in a statement beginning with the words, "God made me."

2. Reflecting upon the statement you just wrote, what might this enable you to do that someone who has a different combination cannot?

3. According to your statement, redefine success in a way that is not based on popularity or profit. Have

you made any progress toward it? If not, what is holding you back?

4. Knowing that we are all a Body that is created with unique parts that are designed to work with each other, how might your gifts help someone else? How might someone else's gifts help you?

5. What is one step you can take to develop satisfaction in the life you have today?

12

"You have no purpose."

All of life is understood by two closely connected but distinct qualities: identity and purpose. Everything is seen not only by "What is it?" or "What is it made of?" but also by "What is it made to do?" Consider how we view the marvels of creation. Stars are not only burning balls of gas, but they are heaven's nightlights. What they are made of helps us understand why they exist. It is the same with trees and plants. They are not only regarded as masses of carbon and water but also as suppliers of oxygen, beauty and shade.

To see something's purpose as an extension of its identity is God's design. The Bible reflects this in a verse that we have been exploring throughout the last two chapters: "For we are God's masterpiece. He has created us anew in Christ Jesus, so we can do the good things he planned for us long ago" (Ephesians 2:10).

So far, we have only focused on the first part of this verse that speaks of identity—you are God's masterpiece. By this point in the book, I hope it is established that you are made intricately and matchlessly in God's image, deemed worthy to be an eternal member of His family in Christ. That is the source of your significance, and it could not be higher.

It is the second part of the verse to which we now turn. It describes that who you are reveals what you do. As God's masterpiece, you are created to "do the good things he planned." Simply put, God created you on purpose for a purpose.

Do you know that purpose? Can you name the reason you exist? If not, you are far from alone. Sadly, most people cannot articulate why they are here. Not because there is no reason, but because most remain on a never-ending search for purpose. The enemy has convinced them that what they do does not matter. Have you ever thought the same? Have you believed that what you have does not rise to the level of making a big enough difference?

This devil-crafted idea is fueled by our media-saturated, celebrity-obsessed culture. We are inundated with the stories of those who break records, invent technologies, find cures, feed small countries, write bestsellers or sing or speak to multitudes. These are people we believe have achieved their purpose because their names or contributions are well-known. Undoubtedly, their lives are inspirational. But they are the exception, not the rule. Most of us will never be number one in our category or influence multitudes. The reality is that if you are waiting for a world-changing thing to do, you will likely be waiting forever.

Years ago, I would have argued with what I just said and taken it as a curse on my potential. When you grow up as I did, believing you are a reject, you look for things that make you stand out. You crave something to do that might make you someone who is important or special. When I confused my doing as the significance of my being, I pursued only what was epic. Purpose was my identity. But as we have seen, that is backward. What you do does not determine who you are; it flows from who you are. Just as God intended.

The Ingredients of Purpose

As Christians, we are called collectively by Jesus to go into all the world, but He never tasked any of us to individually save all the world. Yet that is how many of us approach purpose. We seek to save the world, and then we grow frustrated and hopeless when the abilities and opportunities to do it are lacking. In the pursuit of purpose, the question should not be, "How can I save the world?" but "What do I have to contribute to where I am in the world?"

I read recently, "Lighthouses don't go running all over an island looking for boats to save; they just stand there shining."[1] I love that. You, my friend, are a product of God's craftsmanship made for a good work. Your purpose is not something you have to strive to find or work to possess. Your purpose is to radiate something of Jesus from your unique design that fills a need right where you are. As God's masterpiece, you already have all the ingredients necessary for a deeply meaningful purpose. Let me explain.

Purpose Ingredient #1: What Is in You?

Until my late twenties, I worked in a tech role. I will get into that story later. But as you know, technology evolves at a breakneck pace. Much of what met our needs a year or

185

two ago is outdated today. That is why scalability is more important than ever in the tech industry. What this means is that for products to remain viable beyond the short term, hardware and software designers cannot only consider the needs of today. They must build their products to meet future needs, too.

Electric car manufacturer Tesla is a master of this. Shortly after it launched its Model 3, customers noticed an internal camera pointed at the cabin. Cameras inside and outside of a Tesla are not unusual. Many are there as sensors or to record accidents or vandalism. But this specific cabin camera remained inactive, which drove wild conspiracy theories on the internet. Eventually, Tesla's CEO, Elon Musk, had to clarify that the camera is not some covert spying device. It was included for a day when a Tesla might be used as an unmanned robotaxi. The idea was that the camera will surveil the cabin to help protect the car when there is no human driver. These cars can already drive themselves, so it is not that farfetched. When the world is ready for robotaxis, Tesla is already equipped for the job.

Perhaps it is because of my background that I relate to God as an intelligent designer. I am fascinated by how He wired us, not only for today but also for what is ahead. The Scripture passage we have been exploring reveals that God established His good plans for you well before you were born. At your conception, He equipped you to fulfill those plans. Kind of like a Tesla, you were created with the future in mind. Some of your features have always been evident and active in your life, while others will become evident as they are needed.

Let's consider the evident ones. What are the talents and abilities you have possessed for as long as you can remember?

What are the natural skills that are relatively easy for you to pick up and perform—whether you have mastered them or not?

To aid your thinking, skills generally fit into one of three categories: art, labor or intellectual. Art skills include making music, painting, acting and certain genres of writing. Labor skills are those done by hand such as construction, sports, farming, hairstyling, caretaking, greeting or cooking. Intellectual skills, those such as engineering, programming, teaching and strategizing, are those performed mostly in the mind.

Each ability represents an aspect of God's image. They are divvied out by Him in preparation for a purpose. Consider the men God selected to build Israel's tabernacle at Mount Sinai. He declared that each was gifted with a special skill. Some had wisdom, others were craftsmen, still others had an eye for beauty (see Exodus 31:3–6). A few enjoyed various gifts, but most had only one or two natural talents given to help accomplish God's plan.

Your natural talents and abilities serve a purpose, too, even if you do not have a specific word from God regarding what to do or how to use them. Though that might come in time, you do not need a grand vision to find meaning in what you have. I dare you to identify one skill that does not somehow meet something the world needs right now, whether for its survival or its progress. The arts, for example, offer much-needed enjoyment, but they are also some of the most effective tools for enacting cultural change. Nothing rouses emotions and rallies change more than a song, film, book or sermon. What could be more important to the survival of the world than the labor skills of those who grow and harvest food, build homes, care for children or tend to our physical needs? Finally, I am sure we are all thankful for those who use their minds in ways that bring understanding, organization, order, growth and healing to our lives.

My point is that no skill is coincidental or insignificant. Whatever you have is God-given to support His plans for this moment in history. Do not minimize those skills as meaningless or only something that makes you a livelihood. Embrace and hone your talents as a part of your purpose—but only a part. Because as a Christian, there is more in you than your ability. This leads us to the next ingredient of purpose.

Purpose Ingredient #2: What Drives You?

In 445 BC, a Jewish man named Nehemiah was cupbearer to the King of Persia when he received a troublesome report about his countrymen in Jerusalem (see Nehemiah 1:2–3). The greatest problem, he heard, was that their city wall had not been rebuilt after it had been demolished by invaders more than 140 years earlier. This left Jerusalem susceptible to another devastating attack. Greatly grieved by this, Nehemiah sought the Lord for help. That is when, as he described, God put plans in his heart for Jerusalem. He set out immediately to rebuild the wall himself (see Nehemiah 2:12).

Recalling the biblical definition of heart as the substance of one's inner self, Nehemiah describes that God planted something deep within him—something that became a part of him—that propelled him to act. Today, we call this a passion. Not to be confused with a skill, a passion is not just what you are good at or what you do for a living. A passion is that unshakable something you live for. Often, it is something for which you are willing to sacrifice.

The actor who works two jobs in order to perform on a stage at night does it because of passion. The physician who endured twelve years of school while accruing a couple hundred thousand dollars of debt did it out of passion. It is passion that fuels the stay-at-home parent to care for his or her children instead of climbing a corporate ladder. Passion is that drive in you that acts to quench some internal impulse—not necessarily for a paycheck or any other outcome.

According to Scripture, just as God supplies our skills, He also bestows our passions. As He did with Nehemiah, God gave passions on an individual basis for specific works. Noah had an urgency to build the ark. Moses received the drive to lead Israel out of their oppression. Zerubbabel felt the charge to rebuild Israel's temple. Unquestionably, God still places passions in people to achieve specific purposes. But as Christians, because God's Spirit now lives in us, we do not have to beg Him to give us a passion.

God's heart beats with love for His people. It is His unrelenting desire that every person embraces a relationship with Him (see 1 Timothy 2:4). The spiritual gifts He places within us are passions to serve His children, not simply for our satisfaction (though that is a byproduct). As Peter encouraged, "God has given each of you a gift from his great variety of spiritual gifts. Use them well to serve one another" (1 Peter 4:10).

What drives you? What is that unique, energizing impulse God placed in you that has an impact on someone beyond yourself? If you have difficulty naming something, think through the spiritual gifts we discussed in the last chapter. Are you compelled to stand for truth or challenge the status quo? That is prophecy. Do you come alive with opportunities to reveal new insights or instill age-old principles? That is teaching. Perhaps you love to see people inspired to fulfill their potential. That is encouraging. Maybe you delight in funding missions or faith-based projects or supporting individuals in need. That is giving. If you are energized by casting vision, pioneering new paths or developing a team, that is leadership. And finally, if putting a smile on someone's face lights up yours, that is kindness.

Though there are certain categories of God-given passions, no two inside of any category will look the same. If you and I both possess the gift of teaching, for example, what drives me to teach and what drives you to teach, along with the way we do it, is unique. Uncovering that uniqueness is the most fulfilling part.

Honing Your Passion

It is hardly uncommon for someone to insist, with a bit of desperation in his or her voice, "But I don't know what I'm passionate about!" Oftentimes, people describe something so vague that they have no idea how or where to begin. If that is you, I offer two questions to ask yourself and some steps that you can take.

The first question is, What is the deepest need that God has met in your life? In other words, what obstacle or weakness did God help you overcome or continues to help you face? The second question is, What is the deepest need you see in the world? Chances are that your answer to this question sounds like your answer to the first one. Most likely, the need you see in the world is the need God met in you. When you couple your story with that need, you have both a passion and a people.

These two questions helped me narrow my passion into something specific. I love to help people confront the shame of their struggles with the truth of their identity in Christ. It is what God did in me; therefore, it is what I see is most needed in the world. Still, I did not arrive at the process of how I would answer this need overnight. Nor did it come from a single voice or a vision from heaven. The way that I arrived at my methods might not sound very spiritual, but I have found that it is the most frequent way God uncovers passions or entire purposes in people: I tried things.

Most of us believe that purpose is something that is divinely revealed, like a download from heaven. We believe that it will be accompanied by the road map to fulfill it. In truth, purpose is not usually revealed but is uncovered as you take baby step after baby step in the direction of your passions. At the same time, you trust that God directs those steps (see Psalm 37:23).

Not even the apostle Paul received the details of his purpose all at once. At his conversion on the road to Damascus, he walked away only knowing the next step. All he received from Jesus was, "Get up and go into the city, and you will be told what you must do" (Acts 9:6). As Paul took that step, the next one was given. Then the next. And the next. Sometimes Paul made missteps, but as he stayed in communication with God, he always got back on track.

As I said, I honed my passion in the same way. My faith journey began at sixteen years old. That was step one. I enrolled in a Christian college. That was another step. I sought employment in a few ministries. Those were more steps. In between those steps were smaller but equally clarifying steps. I once attended a weekend intensive to learn street preaching. That step taught me what I did not enjoy! So did my several-month stint teaching children's Sunday school. But the step I took to write my first blog revealed something that energized me, as did the first time I spoke at a church and recorded a message.

What energizes you right now? Do that. Maybe it is as simple as reading a book to your child. Perhaps it is hosting a small group for your church, joining a fitness class at your gym or sharing some spiritual nugget on social media. Take one baby step in the direction of what enlivens you, then do your best to discern God's voice on what is next. Sometimes you will hear it clearly. Many times, you will not. That is okay. Do not be so afraid of a misstep that you do not move at all. The walk of purpose is a walk of faith in which discovering what is not for you is an important part of discovering what is.

Bringing Your Skills and Passions Together for a Purpose

I have been a technology geek for as long as I can remember. Some of my first memories include dissecting our family's first computer and memorizing command lines. Whereas others, like my three older brothers, were content to use the computer for school projects or to play an occasional game, I spent hours at a time absorbing how it worked.

That was during my elementary years. By junior high, the internet went mainstream. It only took a few months after I convinced my parents to subscribe at home that I learned how to code webpages. I built one for my favorite singer. And another for my favorite radio station. None of this did my social status at school any favors. But by the time I was sixteen, my skills did help me land a job as a web programmer for a large religious organization where I specialized in all the new projects. Growing up, I thought my tech talents were the reason for my existence. I believed I was destined to program computers.

Obviously, I am writing to you not as a programmer but a minister. What happened? In short, when I profoundly experienced Jesus in high school, I also experienced new interests and desires that seemed as innate as my computer savvy. I especially felt a fervor for people to know God's truths.

In terms of education, the path I followed—the path toward my skills or the path toward my passion—was made by my parents. In those days, they were not yet on board with my faith, so any notion of a ministry degree was dead on arrival. I did not put up much of a fuss, though. I happily pursued my God-given skills through an undergraduate degree in a computer-related program, while at the same time intensely chasing my passion.

You can do the same. You do not have to completely forsake what you are good at to follow what you love. And while it is great if both your skills and your passions match, for most people, they will not. That is great, too. You will find in time that God will somehow use your skills to serve your passions (and your passions to enrich your skills).

That is what He did with Jesus' disciples. We know that at least four of the twelve made their livelihoods as fishermen. Though Andrew, Peter, James and John initially dropped their nets to follow Jesus, they did not altogether abandon what they grew up doing. They continued to enjoy fishing. But most importantly, the skills of their trade aided their passion for the Gospel. The fishermen became fishers of men. The principles they learned from casting their nets for fish were useful toward casting their nets for a harvest of people.

We explored previously how the apostle Paul's personality suited him for the tenacity he needed to spread the faith. His radical conversion story of pharisee-turned-Christian gave him a level of influence others did not have. It also related Jesus' miracle-working power to people who demanded proof of the faith's validity. But throughout his ministry, Paul maintained a practical skill. He built tents (see Acts 18:3). His occupation not only supported his passion for evangelism, but it also provided a point of contact with people who needed his message. Paul's life is a fitting example of how skills can provide financially for a very different passion. It also demonstrates how God uses every aspect of our gifts in our unique purpose.

This brings me back to my story. After graduating with my computer degree and being employed in technical roles, I grew frustrated that my career had more to do with my skills than my passions. Even after earning a master's degree in biblical studies, I was still called on more for computer advice than spiritual advice. This bothered me intensely, mostly because I believed it minimized my significance. I wanted desperately to be known for something other than building webpages.

What pride blinded me from seeing at the time was that my purpose is not hinged on one or the other. Both my skills and passions prepared me for the uniqueness of this ministry, which fittingly began with a mobile app and internet outreach.

I marvel at how God orchestrated my path to prepare me and provide for what I do today. My skills that were groomed from childhood gave me the knowledge of how to use technology as an effective means to reach people. The experience I gained through my jobs afforded me connections with people who helped bring my ideas to life. And for many years, those jobs also provided the finances to support the ideas. To be sure, the launch of this ministry was not bankrolled by any large donors or family members. Before barely anyone knew my name, God provided all the startup capital through the abilities with which He gifted me. Finally, it was my passion for truth that gave new meaning to my skills. I do not think it is coincidental that today this ministry is largely a media ministry, whereby much of its impact happens through a screen. I am confident this is God's doing, which is why He graced me accordingly.

Please understand, purpose does not have to be about what you do as a full-time profession. But the skills that make you good at what you do can powerfully serve the passion in you. For some, like the disciples, those skills may provide you with experience and abilities that assist your passion. For others, like the apostle Paul, they may provide the funds and opportunities to perform your passion. It is often a little of both.

Whatever the case, be encouraged that you matter. Who you are and what you have are all part of a meaningful purpose that fits a need right where you are. Do not for one second believe that you do not rise to some level of being enough. As one created anew in Christ, you exceed every requirement for significance. Make your every step a step of worthiness and a step of confidence. Not a step *to* purpose but a step *of* purpose.

As I said earlier, as you take steps, sometimes you will make missteps. Sometimes colossal ones. The enemy will use these moments to insist, "You're a failure!" It is his goal to convince you to give up. Let's confront this next.

Speak It!

God created me on purpose for a purpose. He has gifted me with talents, abilities and passions that make a unique imprint. My purpose is not something I achieve or must prove, but it radiates from me right where I am.

Questions for Personal Reflection

1. What has been the greatest obstacle between you and knowing your purpose? What lies created this obstacle?
2. What are the natural talents, abilities and skills that you have possessed since childhood? How have you developed these?
3. What are the interests and desires that energize and drive you? How have these changed or been added to since becoming a Christian?
4. If you could do anything for the rest of your life, what would you do? How might your skills serve this passion?
5. Since reading this chapter, how has your concept of purpose changed? How will it affect your everyday life?

13

LIE:

"You are a failure."

In a letter dated November 13, 1789, Benjamin Franklin composed these now-famous words: "In this world, nothing is certain except death and taxes."[1] His thought has become a modern-day proverb that we do not like and cannot escape even after all these years.

Long before Franklin added his insight to the certainties of life, the apostle Paul shared his own: "For everyone has sinned; we all fall short of God's glorious standard" (Romans 3:23). Like death and taxes, falling short of God's standard is a reality we hate to hear and cannot escape. It means nobody can live perfectly. After all, that is why Jesus came. He understands that "the spirit is willing, but the body is weak" (Matthew 26:41). As long as we are embodied in flesh and live in a world of brokenness, we will fail. We are a work in progress, and that progress is often made two steps forward but one step back.

I know that it stings to hear the inevitability of failure, but it should not. For the Christian, failure is not the problem anymore. Remember that the power of sin is already defeated in Christ; it cannot separate you from God (see Romans 8:38). The devil knows that. That is why failure itself is not his end goal for you. No, he wants it to define you.

Have you heard one of these lines before?

"You did not ace the test. You are a failure."

"You lost your job. You are a failure."

"Your spouse cheated on you. You are a failure."

"Your children got in trouble. You are a failure."

"Your business is not turning a profit. You are a failure."

"You fell again to the same old vice. You are a failure."

Once the enemy gets you to swallow the belief that a mess up means you are messed up, things spiral downward quickly. Negative thoughts leave you wallowing in a pool of your own guilt and shame that influences far more toxic behaviors. The fear that what happened back then will happen again paralyzes you into a comfort zone. Defeat is never found in failure itself, but it is often a byproduct of failure.

Do you currently believe that something from the past or present makes you a failure? If not, the reality of human imperfection means you will likely be confronted with it soon enough. To keep yourself from going down the devil's slippery slope of defeat, remember that failure is an event, it is not a person. It is an incident, but it is not an identity. This means that failure says absolutely nothing about who you are or where you are going.

This is not my opinion alone. It is a thread that runs through the Bible. Select any page of Scripture, and you will likely find someone who has battled some sort of short-coming. You will also notice, however, that these strugglers never out-sinned God's love. No one's mistakes ever changed God's mind about him or her.

We will look at a few examples throughout this chapter, but there is one whose life is particularly instructive regarding failures of the past, present and future. It is Jacob, whose name was changed to Israel. His life includes the two kinds of failure that we all experience at some level. The situation of his birth reflects the kind of failure that is influenced by something not personally chosen. The manipulation of his family represents the kind of failure that is influenced by pride and fleshly desires. His life also reveals the reality of what happens when someone in relationship with God continues to fail. Let's begin with his backstory.

Jacob's Many Failures

For years, Abraham's son Isaac and Isaac's wife, Rebekah, pled with God for children. He answered their prayers even-tually, not with one child but two. Carrying twins cannot be easy, but right from conception, these two made it all the harder—they were at war with each other: "The sons in your womb will become two nations. From the very beginning, the two nations will be rivals. One nation will be stronger than the other; and your older son will serve your younger son" (Genesis 25:23).

The boys came as God had promised. The first one they named Esau. The second they named Jacob. In those days, culture dictated that the firstborn male was entitled to his father's estate and a double portion of whatever inheritance was passed down.[2] This birthright, as it was called, belonged to Esau. But since their father was wealthy, Jacob desperately wanted it.

And Jacob got it. With a bit of manipulation, he seized a moment when Esau was starving and open to doing anything in exchange for a meal. That was Jacob's first failure. Still, he had one more hurdle to overcome before he could officially claim the family inheritance. Back then, they had a kind of safety mechanism in place for things like this. The transfer of a birthright required confirmation from the father through a verbal decree called a blessing.[3]

It is human nature that when you get away with something once, you keep trying it. And Jacob proved he was as human as anyone else. Years later to seal the deal, Jacob capitalized on his father's failing eyesight by dressing so that he felt like Esau. Failure number two. Though this trick also worked, it came with negative consequences. Upon hearing the news, Esau was understandably livid. He was so angry that he plotted to kill his brother. But by the time he could act on his anger, Jacob was long gone. Failure number three.

The Influence of Definitions

Jacob really made a mess of things. While there are no excuses for his choices, there are some influences. First, his name meant one who deceives. Second, his birth order dictated what he could and could not have. It is not surprising, then, that the three failures we count so far in Jacob's life were related to how these labeled him.

Jacob did not choose his name or his birth order, of course. To begin life being defined by something that is not your fault seems unfair, but such is life in our fallen world. To some extent, we all began with something we would not have chosen for ourselves. If you trace the choices you have made, you will likely recognize that the most consequential of choices were a reaction to how those qualities or experiences defined you. Some choices were made to escape pain. Others were made to prove worth. Still others were made to compensate for perceived weakness. How we define ourselves affects what we do.

The first three decades of my life were largely characterized by this. By now, you have heard many of my stories. But there is one from the seventh grade that specifically serves as a microcosm of how definitions lead to defeat. It all goes back to my timid, insecure nature as a child. It held me back not only socially and athletically but also academically. That is why, at least through elementary, most of my grades were mediocre. Especially in math.

Although I had battled plenty of other labels from many other things, my lack of ability in math was never one of them. That changed in the seventh grade when the administration made a foolish decision. Rather than divide our class of fifty into two random groups as they had before, they decided to segregate us based solely on math ability. This meant that all year, every subject was taken with the same students of the same math level. Officially, administrators named the two classes "701" and "702." To everyone else, however, it was "7-0-1" and "7-0-DUMB."

At school that year, an inadequacy in one area defined every other area. Looking back, I realize the label affected not only the classes I took but also my thoughts and behaviors. I struggled a lot that year both in other subjects and with friendships. Right at the dawning of adolescence, being labeled "dumb" was demoralizing and debilitating to my growth. How I was defined affected what I did.

Not only do definitions influence what we do, but they also argue for what we cannot do and should not do. In Scripture, Moses' speech impediment established him as a kind of failure. While we do not know for sure, he probably faced ridicule because of it. Undoubtedly, this innate weakness labeled him in his own mind. That is why, as we have already explored in past chapters, when God called him to lead His people out of Egypt, he insisted he would fail: "O Lord, I'm not very good with words. . . . I get tongue-tied, and my words get tangled" (Exodus 4:10).

What happened to you, what someone said about you, what you experienced because of your own choices—none of those things need to define you or dictate your future. You have a greater definition that was given by your Creator, the only One who has any real authority to define you. All throughout the Bible, from kings to commonfolk, you will find that a word from God is always the answer to failure.

That is what changed Moses and filled him with new-found confidence. God interrupted his "I'm doomed to fail because . . ." monologue with one of those rhetorical questions He is known to use to quiet a complaint: "Who makes a person's mouth? Who decides whether people speak or do not speak. . . . Is it not I, the LORD?" (verse 11). He did not need to say much more. This single question told Moses, "I'm the One who designed you and defined you, and you will succeed as I determined." And he did. With God's assurance and help, Moses fulfilled his calling and defied all his labels and limits.

In my case, God's Word changed me, too. Not just to overcome the "dumb" label from seventh grade, but to overcome all those labels that I and others had put on me over the years. When I discovered God's truths at sixteen years old, even though I did not know everything instantly about my new identity in Christ, I knew enough to know that my past and inadequacies did not have to hold me back. I determined that I would not be labeled dumb anymore. By the time I graduated from high school (from a different school with quadruple the students), I finished in the top ten of my class. As with Moses, God's definitions influenced my success.

As we return to Jacob's story, we will see the same. A single word from God altered the course of his life. Not only that, but why it happened, how it happened and what happened later provide profound insights about getting over future failures. Let's continue.

Jacob's Identity Change

As many of us have experienced, what you run from catches up with you eventually. I suspect there is a spiritual reason for that. Peace does not come from ignoring a past regret or a present struggle. It does not come from ignoring that you have wronged someone or that someone has wronged you. It comes from confronting those things.

It was the same for Jacob. Years later, he got word that his brother was drawing near. Struggling with what to do, Jacob sent his entourage ahead while he stayed back for an evening of soul-searching. Jacob's thoughts were not all he struggled with that night. Suddenly, from out of nowhere, a man showed up for a fight. And not just an arm wrestle. The two brawled until Jacob's hip was pulled out of socket. Painful as it might have been, he would not back down: "I will not let you go unless you bless me" (Genesis 32:26).

203

Recall that in those days, a blessing was not merely a prayer spoken over someone. It was a verbal decree that conferred meaning upon someone. Jacob was about to get far more than he asked for.

To his bold demand, the man asked, "What is your name?"

He replied, "Jacob." Then came the blessing. "Your name will no longer be Jacob," the man told him. "From now on you will be called Israel, because you have fought with God and with men and have won" (see Genesis 32:27–28).

There is much more here than what meets the eye. Jacob met no mere man that night. At perhaps his lowest point, just before he was about to face the consequences of his failures, he met God. When God asked his name, it was not because He did not know. I believe God was going after his labels.

"Who do others say you are?"

"What has your past dictated to you?"

"How have your failures defined you?"

Jacob's response, therefore, effectively acknowledged, "I am one who deceives." This had to be as humbling of a moment as getting his hip pulled out of socket. But this humbling made him ripe for what was next. Confessing the old, he was ready for the new. That is the moment God changed his identity. And with that new identity, He gave him a new destiny that was not dictated by anything but His Word.

Getting Over Failure

In each story that we have explored so far, we see that victory over a failure always came through a word from God in a meeting with God. Nothing positive happens by ignoring mistakes. Failure should always drive us to Jesus.

Our salvation was a meeting with God whereby we surrendered our sin nature and received Jesus' righteousness. Our new righteous definition supersedes all others. But we tend to forget it, especially after a failure. That is why God continues to invite us back. He wants us to encounter Him. A moment as this one is called repentance, which is key to getting over failure.

I know that the word *repentance* can come with considerable baggage. This baggage can come because we make it performance focused and dependent on personal willpower. But before repentance touches your behaviors, it must first touch your mind and permeate your beliefs. Remember, it is right believing that leads to right behaving, not the other way around.

Repentance, which is *metanoia* in Greek, is primarily a change of mind. On the Day of Pentecost when Peter urged the Jewish people to "repent and be baptized, every one of you, in the name of Jesus Christ for the forgiveness of your sins" (Acts 2:38 NIV), it was a call to change their minds about who Jesus was and go from unbelief to belief. Consistently throughout the New Testament, it is this changed belief that results in salvation.

That is for an unbeliever. For believers, repentance is not about believing in Jesus all over again. It is a beautiful act of coming humbly (not fearfully or with shame) before God to surrender those failures and their definitions, and then being renewed in mind and posture to God's ways and truths, particularly to who He says you are.

If you need to, take a moment to do that right now. Imagine yourself placing the labels and limits of your weaknesses, the words of others and your own wrong turns, decisions and motives into the hands of Jesus. Tell Him, "Lord, I don't want this anymore," or "Lord, I don't want to do this anymore." Imagine Him—with a look of love in His eyes—gladly taking it from you. Now receive His blessing. God says, *You are not identified by your failures. You are defined as righteous, loved and accepted.* Be renewed to the truth that, in Christ, God sees you in a state of perfection and not imperfection, in celebration and not condemnation, in success and not failure.

Perfection Is Not the Goal

After his encounter with God, Jacob was so moved that he named the place where it happened, Peniel, which means "face of God" (see Genesis 32:30). But then he moved on, sure of God's Word. That is what you must do, too. After you accept what God says, you need to begin to walk in your new identity. This does not mean that you strive to be worthy of it, but rather to rest in and enjoy the certainty of it. As we have already covered, there is no way to walk perfectly enough to be worthy of His righteousness. You will fail if you try.

It is common to think that an experience like the one that Jacob had with God would make a person nearly infallible, but it does not. In all the life-changing encounters with God that we see throughout Scripture, not a single person lived perfectly ever after. Jacob certainly did not.

Sure, he possessed a new desire to do what was right, which is why he went immediately to make peace with his brother. That is the power of repentance. Still, Jacob later deceived again. After promising Esau that he would meet him back at his home in Seir, Jacob continued to a different town. But his new failure did not undo his identity change. It did not convert him back to, "Jacob, the one who deceives."

No, despite all of his future failures, he remained Israel, the man through whom God established a nation that many years later produced Jesus.

In a world where everything is judged by performance, it may be perplexing to understand how someone could keep his title or position after he fails so many times. But remember, your identity in Christ is more than a title or position. It is your nature—the very core of who you are. The defining theme in the stories of so many of our favorite Bible heroes is how God's decisions about them withstood their most glaring and repeated failures. There are so many beyond Jacob that we could recount. King David, for example, even after falling to adultery, remained known by God as a "man after my own heart" (1 Samuel 13:14; Acts 13:22).

In the New Testament, perhaps the most obvious example is the apostle Peter. Born as Simon, his name was changed to Peter during an encounter with Jesus (see John 1:42). Again, this was not only a name change but also an identity change. Peter means "rock." But not any ole rock. Jesus added purpose to it: "Upon this rock I will build my church, and all the powers of hell will not conquer it" (Matthew 16:18).

Real as this was, Peter was not always rocklike. Most notably, on three occasions after Jesus' arrest, he denied knowing Him. Yet through it all, Jesus' words endured. Peter stood boldly on the Day of Pentecost to preach a message that led three thousand people to Christ. That was a great day for him. But other not-so-great days followed, such as when Paul chastised him for being cowardly (see Galatians 2:11–13). You see, even for those closest to Jesus, success ebbs and flows. Yet their new identities stay rock-solid.

In highlighting these stories, I do not mean to glory in failure or advocate that you live a sloppy, undisciplined life.

207

As we already discussed in chapter 6, failures—especially those of the sinful kind—have natural consequences. In the least, they can open you up to more battles. Why would you ever want to purposefully fail?

Still, backward as it might sound, it is a devil-crafted lie to insist that it is possible to live perfectly. If perfection is your goal, you will only remain on the roller coaster of shame and remain grief stricken every time you stumble. Rather, set your goal to live joyfully in the truth and power of who you are in Christ. When you mess up, repeat the repentance process. Not so that you might have a chance to be restored to righteousness, but so that your mind will be renewed to the righteousness you already have in Christ.

The Value of a Mistake

Failure is never the final answer when it is surrendered to God. Anything placed in His hands can be repurposed into something of priceless value. We have this remarkable promise that "God causes everything to work together for the good of those who love God" (Romans 8:28). Failures are particularly capable of that. A home improvement project, of all things, taught me how.

It was only two years after I moved into my first home that I decided I could no longer stand the vinyl flooring in the entrances, kitchen and bathrooms. I wanted it all ripped out and replaced with tile. But I had two problems. First, I was too cheap to hire a professional to do the work. Second, as I divulged a few chapters ago, I am not much of a handyman. That combination does not go together well. So when a far more experienced friend offered to help, I jumped at the opportunity to begin.

We started by sharpening our skills in a small entryway. What we failed to consider is that home foundations are notoriously unlevel, and cutting tile to go around door frames is an art that is not developed over night. Suffice it to say that what should have taken an evening to complete took five days, and it was accompanied with backaches, blisters and blood!

After a couple of weeks of rest and reflection, my friend and I both reconvened with the same realization that we were hopelessly in over our heads. The remaining areas were too complicated for a couple of amateurs. I had no other choice but to swallow my pride and pony up the cash to hire a professional.

Not even an hour into the contractor's work, I realized the difference that thirty years of experience makes. So much difference, in fact, that I considered the difficult decision of having him tear up and redo all the work we had slaved over.

I mulled the idea over, all the while complaining to God that with the time and tools already invested, the project would end up costing me more than if I had hired it out from the start. Shortly into my protest, I felt God deposit a word into me that made up my mind. *Lessons learned are often expensive, but in the end, they are worth the cost.*

Indeed, as we have all experienced, the mistakes, failures and wrong turns we make in life are costly in all kinds of ways. Some cost precious time. Others cost innocence, relationships and, yes, money. Unquestionably, in and of themselves, mistakes are not worth anything. The worth is found in the redemption that follows when you take the failure to the throne of grace, ask God to teach you something from it and do something with it. It is the character that is built, the testimony that is told and the healing that happens that make the lesson learned worth the cost it took to learn it.

In the case of my flooring project, not only did I receive valuable lessons for the future (mostly, not to do these things myself!), but the story of my failure also made its way into my messages and this book where it now encourages others. That is redemption. That is God turning my bad into something for good.

Your failures of whatever source and significance can do the same. If you place them in God's hands, He will take them and remake them into something that serves both you and others. As only He can, God will transform those obstacles that caused you to fall into the steppingstones of tomorrow's strength, wisdom and courage. He will rearrange those setbacks to be setups for your faith, finances, relationships and career. He will use the lessons of what you went through to be someone else's guide to breakthrough. Yes, in some incredible way, God will use what the enemy meant for your defeat to defeat the enemy, instead. Determine to use your failures for his defeat.

As we turn to the final chapter, let's talk about your weaknesses, specifically what to do about the ones you fear are in the way of fulfilling all God has for you.

Speak It!

I am not a failure. I am defined by Jesus' perfection and success; therefore, my future is not based upon my mistakes. I will live joyfully and authentically in Christ, knowing that God is working all things for my good.

Questions for Personal Reflection

1. How have failures in the past been used to shame you or convince you to stay in a comfort zone?
2. Can you identify any definitions that have influenced your negative choices? Why do you think they made you act accordingly?
3. Are there failure-based identities that you need to surrender to God? Take a moment to do that. Then, what are some truths about your new identity with which you need to renew your mind?
4. How does the reality that God does not expect you to live perfectly rid shame and produce more victory in your life?
5. What lessons have you learned from past mistakes that have made you better today? How might God continue to use your past and present failures for good?

14

LIE:

"You are disqualified."

If I could listen to a replay of my life's prayers, I would hear a lot of these kinds of pleas. They would begin with, "How can I, Lord," and be followed by

"... when I don't have the money?"

"... when I don't have the energy?"

"... when I don't have the connections?"

"... when I don't have the ability?"

If there is one predominant insecurity that I have battled at every stage of life, it is that something in me or about me means that I do not measure up. I have feared that some weakness could disqualify me.

There is so much I could recount. In school, I feared my awkward and clumsy athletic ability meant I was not man enough. You have already heard how my introverted personality made me suppose I was not fit for ministry. I thought being unmarried at 35 kept me out of the pastor's club—at least the Protestant one. I once believed my 5'7" height and small-shirt-size build was not commanding enough to be a real leader—whatever that means.

I know that some of what I mentioned sounds trivial, even silly. But that is how it goes with weaknesses. They do not have to make sense or be real to be limiting. They just must be felt. As you know by now, the devil takes every opportunity to interpret something in your life as a reason that you cannot, you should not, you will not or you are not. Weaknesses might be the grand Pooh-Bah of them all, the fodder for every lie we have explored.

They do not, of course, always lie about *everything* we should not do. As you now know, it is best that I do not remodel your home, paint you a picture or sing you a song. I mean, I could try, but trust me, you would not want me to. I am sure you also have your own list of things you should not attempt.

I am not talking about areas in which we are not already gifted or called. I am talking about the ability to work within our skills and passions, to flourish within our purposes, to fulfill our dreams and to be used by God. Those are where our weaknesses can seem most disqualifying.

Moving forward, the question we should ask ourselves is not do we have weaknesses, but what do we do with them? More specifically, how do we neutralize their influence and take away their power to shame us? The answer is as unique as you are.

What to Do with Your Weaknesses

When it comes to what to do about a weakness, I waffled for so long back and forth between two either/or options that you have likely heard before: fix or embrace. Both have their support in Scripture and their success stories, which all add to the confusion. Do you cling to the hope of change and do everything in your power to foster it, or do you let go and somehow learn to live with it? Your answer might be different based on the day, who you listen to or what you read. Mine was.

I could point you to plenty of Bible verses that make it seem as if the issues in our lives can be resolved with enough discipline and willpower. No doubt, as I have shared from my life, contending with spiritual disciplines such as Scripture meditation, fasting and prayer can absolutely change us. Lifestyle disciplines like diet, exercise and using internet accountability software can, too.

The danger with the fix-it solution, however, is that it tends to minimize faith to being nothing more than a glorified self-help program that tends toward legalism—as I experienced in the first decade of my Christianity. Since nobody can perform perfectly, when you inevitably fail, all the blame and burden goes back on you. The ups and downs only keep you shackled to shame and condemnation.

The other problem is that no matter how hard you try, you cannot fix everything. If that is not already obvious in your life, we can see it demonstrated in the life of perhaps the most influential Christ follower, the apostle Paul.

If there was anyone that I would guess had both the willpower and the divine favor to overcome a difficulty, it would be Paul. Raised to be a Pharisee, he had the discipline to follow the law as much as anyone could. As a Christian, miracles and deliverance characterized his ministry. Yet despite all his pedigree and power, he battled a weakness that would not go away. A "thorn in the flesh," as he called it (see 2 Corinthians 12:7).

The source of Paul's thorn keeps preachers and scholars swirling with speculation. Some believe it was a physical ailment or disability. Some say it was the harsh words and accusations of his detractors. Others contend it was an annoying personality trait that resulted in rejection. I have gone down the rabbit hole of trying to figure out his thorn at least a time or two. You can Google it if you would like, but I will save you the time: nobody really knows. The only clue Paul gave is that it was a messenger from Satan. That could be anything from a headache to a co-worker!

Like I said, if anyone could resolve an issue, my money would be on Paul. And I do not think it is unreasonable to assume he tried. We know he pleaded with God to take it away three times. I consider that a fix-it method. I am surprised he only begged three times. Until I got to the place I am about to explain, there were battles that I asked God to remove at least a thousand times. Surely you can relate.

In Paul's case, all his begging, pleading and whatever else he attempted did not change a thing. God did not take it away. Paul recounted, "Each time he said, 'My grace is all you need. My power works best in weakness'" (verse 9). I love how Paul is sure to note "each time." I imagine the following scene unfolding.

At first, Paul is on his knees at the edge of his bed, knuckles white from his tightly folded hands. He implores, "Lord, this is too tough. I can't fight this anymore. Take this from me!"

Then he hears a simple whisper that says, *My grace is all you need.*

"No," Paul mutters to himself in what he thinks is righteous indignation. "That can't be God's voice. He wouldn't want me to have this! Thorn, go, in Jesus' name!" Nothing changes.

"I won't accept this," Paul resolves right before he decides it is time to bring in his prayer warriors. After binding and rebuking every spirit they can name, Paul hears yet again a quiet, heavenly voice.

Grace.

Yes, I put lots of words into the mind and mouth of Paul. Or maybe I projected myself onto him. Scripture only gives us a glimpse into his exchange with God, but I am sure it lasted more than a moment and was accompanied with plenty of emotion, frustration and confusion.

As humans, we desire the removal of every obstacle, everything that is painful, and all things that are abnormal. That is natural. And as long as we are not striving to fix ourselves in order to gain something from God, I think it is fine—even wise sometimes—to try. But more often than not, God's response to our most fervent efforts and prayers is the same as it was to Paul: "My grace is all you need. My power works best in weakness."

I know that grace is one of those words that sounds inspirational, but we often do not know what to do with it. If that is the case for you—that you do not know what to do with grace—then you are on the right track. As we have seen through this book, grace is not about what you do. It is the acceptance and approval of God despite what you do. As a believer, you do not have to strive to possess acceptance and approval, because you already have them in Christ. Grace means that you are right with God even in your weaknesses. Confidence in that truth takes away the substance of the enemy's accusations. That is huge enough.

But grace is also God's empowerment despite your lack of power. It is showing up and being surrendered to God as you are, and then watching Him work through who you are. This is the embracing option, and it is where Paul arrived eventually. He even got to the point of boasting, "I take pleasure in my weaknesses" (verse 10). That might sound strange to you, but after landing in the same place, I can attest there is an uncanny freedom, even advantage, that comes from embracing your weaknesses instead of forever trying to fix them. Toward the end of this chapter, we will get to what that looks like.

Do you feel unsatisfied by the either/or approach? I do. The fix-it method is not always healthy, nor is it entirely possible. And in some cases, the embrace-it option might be more detrimental than it is helpful. Should you simply settle with things such as addictions and other destructive behaviors? That cannot be God's will, either.

While scouring for wisdom on how to counsel someone who was struggling, I stumbled upon a much more satisfying solution than the either/or option. It is hidden in plain sight in Paul's conclusion to his thorn in the flesh: "For when I am weak, then I am strong" (verse 10).

Do you see it? I didn't until more recently. For years, I somehow always misread this verse as, "For when I am weak, then *He* is strong." While that is certainly true, those are not Paul's words. He said, "*I am* weak, then *I am* strong."[1]

In Paul's two "I am" statements, you can find the answer for what to do with your weaknesses. It is not always weakness *or* strength, but weakness *and* strength—embracing *and* fixing. In that order.

Rather than running off—as I did in the early days of my faith—and attempting to use every spiritual principle in the book to fix yourself, begin with the realization that it is okay to have imperfections. Your weaknesses change nothing about how much God loves you. Some, however, could get in the way of how much you love God. Some could result in pain and grief that you do not have to battle. Some could open you needlessly up to the enemy's attacks.

If that is the case, then with the tools, resources and power that God provides through grace, try whatever you would like in order to change. Memorize those Scripture verses. Go on that fast. Proceed through the twelve steps to deliverance. Then leave the results to Him, knowing that whatever happens, you remain His child, His delight and His masterpiece.

Does all that sound more open-ended than you hoped? Maybe a bit messy? Such is the Christian life. There is rarely a one-size-fits-all solution to anything. Part of your journey is to work with God to find what is right for you. Let's talk about that.

Finding Your Custom Solution

In saying that you should find what is right for you, I do not mean that truth is different for different people. What I mean is that a weakness that God fixes in one person He might ask another to embrace. That is never because God wants someone to suffer, but because a weakness could open opportunities that would not be available without it. If that gives you pause, stick with me. What I am about to say from now through the end of the chapter will explain this.

For starters, many of the qualities that we think are imperfections are part of our unique design. God is not going to change something He crafted in the first place, regardless of how ostracized it makes you. Take my natural personality type, for example. I told you that for years I worked hard to change it through prayer, exercises and deliverance. I think one time I even commanded, "Introversion, go in

219

Jesus' name!" I was positive that my quiet demeanor was of the devil!

Where did I get that idea? Not from Scripture. I got it from a culture that celebrates extroversion. I got it from the expectations of others. I got it from the pain of rejection I sometimes suffered because of it. Yet being an introvert is God's design for me. Look to the stories of many of your favorite Bible heroes, and you will see that His designs do not always make someone popular or comfortable. But until you know better or you hear from God, it is easy to mistake them for flaws. You can find yourself battling to change things God is not interested in changing.

Still, they might need to be refined. In our fallen world, even God's designs get broken. Every gift has its vulnerabilities that can be exploited by the enemy. Talking about the personality types, introverts may be prone to isolation or social anxiety, while extroverts may be prone to an unhealthy need for acceptance.[2]

In my case, the extreme shyness in my childhood was not what God desired. So when I began to learn about my identity in Christ, I discerned what I needed to address and what I needed to embrace. With God's help, I took steps to shed the fear and grow in confidence. But I am still an introvert.

Perhaps you are wondering, "What about sinful behaviors that clearly aren't God's designs?" The truth is, dealing with sin in a way that is lasting is also a custom process that happens through relationship with God. He provides the empowerment, encouragement and steps for you to take at the right time. Do your part, of course, to limit sin's influence in your life. This is not an excuse to be lazy, but you should know that the burden of battling sin is not yours alone. It is a partnership with grace—grace to give you strength you do not naturally have, and grace to pick you up when you fall.

Again, messy. While I cannot give you a surefire formula for knowing exactly what to fix, what to embrace and how to go about it, I can offer a prayer to help kick-start the process.

Father, help me know what to contend for and what to let go of. If it is Your will to remove this weakness in me, then give me the grace to do what I need to do, and help me to trust You to do what I cannot. But if it is to embrace it, then I ask You to empower me with Your grace to be obedient with it. Whatever Your plan, Lord, may nothing shame or limit me. In Jesus' name, Amen.

God Is Calling *You*

Whatever God's plan is, you are qualified for whatever God has called you to in this season. I think about Gideon in the Old Testament. He lived at a time when God's people were surrounded and terrorized by enemies known as the Midianites. Gideon was hardly someone who was gifted with grit. In fact, he was so intimidated by them that he did his work while hiding inside an underground pit.

Much to his shock, right in the place of his fear, the Lord appeared and called out to him, "Mighty hero, the LORD is with you" (Judges 6:12). Gideon must have snickered, "Yeah, right." There was nothing heroic about his situation.

But God wasn't joking. He instructed, "Go with the strength you have, and rescue Israel from the Midianites" (verse 14).

In a response remarkably reminiscent of Moses, Gideon dared to question the Lord: "How can I rescue Israel? My clan is the weakest in the whole tribe . . . and I am the least in my entire family!" (verse 15).

I suggest you read the story for yourself, but in short, after a few tests to ensure that he had really heard from God, Gideon went. As most of us would, he first tried to fix his weakness. He built a massive army of 32,000 warriors. But after some back-and-forth with the Lord, he was left with merely three hundred men. So yes, Gideon strengthened himself to take on God's task, but mostly he had to embrace his weakness and let God's grace do the work.

As you probably guessed, God's custom solution succeeded. Gideon and his super-small army conquered their enemies. They did not battle in the usual way with javelins, spears and swords. They battled with rams' horns and clay jars.

The point of Gideon's example is this: God does not consider a person's qualities to determine if they are qualified for His assignments. In the natural, Gideon was far from mighty, much less a hero. God knew this. Since the issues of Gideon's life were not a surprise to Him, they were not a factor in His decision to use Gideon. That is why God did not say, "Let me know when you're prepared enough or ready enough." God's call was not about Gideon being enough of anything. No, He said, "Go with the strength you have. . . . I am sending you" (verse 14).

Hear that for yourself. God is not waiting for you to overcome every weakness before you are good enough to be used by Him. He says instead, "Go in who you are and what you have. I will make up the difference." Even with all your quirky qualities, God is sending you. With all your faults and failures, God is sending you. In your imperfections, God is sending you. In Him, you are equipped for whatever He asks you to do.

▌ Purpose in Your Imperfections

Gideon's obedience to God while he was still weak placed him into what is known as the Faith Hall of Fame (see Hebrews 11). It is a kind of Who's Who of imperfect people who achieved incredible feats. They did these not despite their weaknesses but because of them. After chronicling those like Noah, Abraham, Rahab and David, the author of Hebrews concludes, "They shut the mouths of lions, quenched the flames of fire, and escaped death by the edge of the sword. Their weakness was turned to strength" (Hebrews 11:33–34).

I need to emphasize that last line, "turned to strength." This does not mean weakness was replaced by strength. It means the very weakness itself became a strength. Does that sound implausible or impossible in your circumstance? Are you convinced there is no way that what you battle could ever be anything of value? Not so fast. Both Scripture and history are full of people whose weaknesses, when empowered by grace, became their unfair advantage. An entire book could be written on that. But here are at least a few of the ways this looks.

A weakness can lead you to having a great impact on others.

All his life, a friend of mine battled ADHD—not a small dose of it, either. His family nicknamed him Tigger (as in Winnie the Pooh) because of how much he bounced around in both his body and his mind. He was not officially diagnosed until after college. That is why, after my friend attempted a class paper, one of his professors bluntly asked, "Do you have a learning disability?"

Not surprisingly, the candid words of his professor further highlighted what he already believed disqualified him from his aspiration to be a high school teacher. He started taking medication, which helped his focus, but it did not help enough for him to be able to create cohesive lesson plans, much less follow them.

Yet in his weakness, he went on to become a teacher of the year in his school district. You see, the weakness that still earns him low marks for lesson planning and organization is also what makes him a creative, out-of-the-box teacher the students love and respect.

I am convinced that my friend would not have as big of an impact without his so-called weakness. And he is hardly alone in that. History is filled with similar stories of those whose weaknesses and failures led them to an opportunity they never would have had without it. I think of how Thomas Edison came to invent the lightbulb. Or how Oprah found her passion for interviewing. In God's way, it is often the very things we think limit us that become what make us most successful.

A weakness can create a connection and compassion to help others.

I have heard it said that where the serpent has bitten you is where you have your greatest authority. What this means is that your struggles reveal the areas where you can help others the most.

There are two reasons for this. First, in most people's minds, experience is what gives someone the credibility to speak about a topic. Right now, nobody will listen to me about how to raise children. I only have theory with no real experience. But on the subject of insecurity, well, I speak

from plenty of experience with that. That is why you made
it this far in this book. I trust my stories created a connection with you. I am sure it is the same with the other books
you read or podcasts you listen to. Are not those that are the
most helpful and moving created by people who share from
the deep wells of what they have been through?

I am not suggesting that you should expose your every
weakness to everyone, but being able to speak from experience and with vulnerability connects you in a way that takes
your words past people's minds and into their hearts.

Second, weakness provides a compassion that often com-
pels people to help others. Perhaps the greatest example
comes from Jesus. He was not weak in the sense that He
did anything wrong, but Scripture does say that He "understands our weaknesses, for he faced all of the same testings
we do" (Hebrews 4:15). Jesus understood what it is like to
be hungry, angry, tempted, betrayed, criticized and so much
more. That draws us to Him all the more. It also created a
compassion in Him for the plight of being human. We see
the result of this in the story of Jesus feeding the five thousand. When He saw the crowd of broken, desperate people,
compassion rose in Him. This compelled Him to help them
(see Matthew 14:14).

I am definitely not Jesus, but I have experienced the similar
effect of receiving compassion from weakness. After I began
to embrace and understand God's grace in my own brokenness, I started to extend God's grace for the brokenness of
others. I cannot overestimate how that has helped me and
others. For one, I find it easier to forgive because I know of
what I have been forgiven. I also have significantly deeper
insight that brings life instead of legalism to my teaching
and counsel. And though I am not perfect in this, when I

see people as fellow hurting human beings, I have far more mercy and patience for the challenges and setbacks of their journeys. Undoubtedly, my weaknesses make my ministry far more effective than if I did not have them. Yours can do the same, if you will decide to let God use them.

A weakness can demonstrate the reality of God's power and goodness.

Some years ago, while wrestling with why Paul would prefer to boast in weakness over miraculous experiences, the Lord dropped some strange words into me.

He said, *My grace in weakness is equally as miraculous as removal of the weakness.*

"How can that be?" I questioned. "What is miraculous about something that doesn't change?" His response is what forever altered my thoughts about weakness, even battles. And it fittingly encapsulates the message of this book.

Grace is the miracle of My presence upholding human frailty with a strength to press through what the enemy meant to subdue.

You might need to ponder that for a few minutes as I did. You see, if you think of the stories that we often put on display, they are almost always those of 180-degree change, healing or deliverance. And while I am not minimizing those kinds of experiences, do you know what are often more helpful to people? The stories of those who remain faithful to God amid difficulties that do not go away. People such as Gideon and Moses who persevere in weakness and who demonstrate hope to other imperfect people. People who show us that their issues do not have to define them, limit them or disqualify them. They essentially say, "The same God who upholds me will also uphold you." To me, that is a message far more encouraging and relatable than only stories about obstacles that are removed suddenly. I think that is why Paul decided, "I will boast only about my weaknesses" (2 Corinthians 12:5).

Please understand that while God is not the creator of imperfections, He is the redeemer of them. And if you let Him, He will repurpose whatever you face into something that makes the devil regret the day that he messed with you. He will use your life as a living illustration of the fact that all things can work together for good. Trust me, there is nothing more satisfying than that. And there is nothing for which you are more qualified. For that, God does not need your strength. He just needs your surrender.

Your Ultimate Victory

As we come to a close, let me bring you back to what I said in the first part of this book. To shut up the devil does not mean that you somehow keep him from talking. I can assure you that the enemy will return from time to time with his slanderous lies. And he will continue to use all the ways you are broken and imperfect as the substance of them. That is all he has.

But now when he does, you don't have to be plunged into despair or endless mind games. You now know the truth that victory does not mean the absence of weakness, struggle or difficulty. No, ultimate victory is knowing that none of those issues define you. It is the confidence that God's Word is more real than how you feel, what you fear or the ways that you fail.

My friend, you are a child of God who is meticulously handcrafted in His image, accepted and set apart in Christ for a unique purpose that only you can fulfill. From this moment on—in your mind, with your mouth and with all your heart—never back down from the magnitude of everything that this means about you. For nothing shuts up the devil and shuts down your battles more than the certainty that because of grace

You are loved.
You are right.
You are complete.
You are valuable.
You are good enough.

Speak It!

I am not disqualified by the ways I am imperfect, the weaknesses I possess or the battles I face. God's grace qualifies and empowers me to fulfill His plans. In Christ, I am loved, I am right, I am complete, I am valuable and I am good enough.

Questions for Personal Reflection

1. Think about the qualities that you consider to be imperfections or weaknesses. How has the enemy used them to shame or limit you?

2. In what weakness do you sense that God is saying to embrace it and not fix it? In what weakness do you sense He asks you to contend for change? Why?

3. In what ways has a weakness shifted you to do something that ended up having more of an impact with it than without it?
4. How might the story of your weakness be used by God to offer hope and encouragement to others?
5. Reflecting upon everything you discovered in this book, what is your greatest takeaway? How will it influence your life?

Notes

Chapter 1 The Slanderer

1. Editorial Team, "How Fast Can a Lion Run?," Africa Freak, August 26, 2019, https://africafreak.com/how-fast-can-a-lion-run.

2. Strong's Concordance, "1228. Diabolos," Bible Hub, 2021, https://biblehub.com/greek/1228.htm.

3. "Slander," Lexico, 2021, https://www.lexico.com/en/definition/slander.

4. Brendan D'mello, "What Makes a Lion's Roar So Loud and Intimidating?," Science ABC, February 1, 2021, https://www.scienceabc.com/nature/secret-behind-lions-roar.html.

5. "Predatory Behaviour," Lion Alert, January 8, 2020, https://lionalert.org/predatory-behaviour/.

6. The source of this quote cannot be verified because it has been attributed to many people throughout history. For a discussion on this quote, see "Watch Your Thoughts," Quote Investigator, January 10, 2013, https://quoteinvestigator.com/2013/01/10/watch-your-thoughts/.

Chapter 2 The Secret Strategy against Your Mind

1. Strong's Concordance, "3053. Logismos," Bible Hub, 2021, https://biblehub.com/greek/3053.htm.

Chapter 3 Mastering Your Mind

1. Julie Bartucca, "The Most Complicated Object in the Universe," UConn Today, March 16, 2018, https://today.uconn.edu/2018/03/complicated-object-universe/#.

2. Kendra Cherry, "How Experience Changes Brain Plasticity," Very Well Mind, February 3, 2021, https://www.huffpost.com/entry/the-10-fundamentals-of-re_b_9625926.

3. Debbie Hampton, "The 10 Fundamentals of Rewiring Your Brain," HuffPost, June 2016, https://www.huffpost.com/entry/the-10-fundamentals -of-re_b_9625926.

4. Thai Nguyen, "10 Proven Ways to Grow Your Brain: Neurogenesis and Neuroplasticity," HuffPost, June 2016, https://www.huffpost.com/entry/10 -proven-ways-to-grow-yo_b_10374730.

5. Dr. Jun Lin and Dr. James Tsai, "The Optic Nerve and Its Visual Link to the Brain," DiscoveryEye.org, March 12, 2015, https://discoveryeye.org /optic-nerve-visual-link-brain/.

6. Jill Suttie, "How to Overcome Your Brain's Fixation on Bad Things," *Greater Good Magazine*, January 13, 2020, https://greatergood.berkeley .edu/article/item/how_to_overcome_your_brains_fixation_on_bad_things.

7. "Metamorphoo," BibleStudyTools.com, 2021, https://www.biblestudy tools.com/lexicons/greek/nas/metamorphoo.html.

8. Fit4D, "The Neuroscience of Behavior Change," StartUp Health, August 8, 2017, http://healthtransformer.co/the-neuroscience-of-behavior-change -bcb567fa83c1.

Chapter 4 The Mind-Mouth Connection

1. Eugene E. Carpenter and Philip W. Comfort, "Meditate," *Holman Treasury of Key Bible Words: 200 Greek and 200 Hebrew Words Defined and Explained* (Nashville: Broadman and Holman, 2000), 123.

2. Jeremy Thompson, "Heart," *Bible Sense Lexicon: Dataset Documentation* (Bellingham, Wash.: Faithlife, 2015).

3. Fit4D, "The Neuroscience of Behavior Change," StartUp Health, August 8, 2017, https://healthtrasnfromer.co/theneauroscience-of-behavior-change -bcb567fa83c1.

4. Andrew Newberg and Mark Waldman, "Why This Word Is So Dangerous to Say or Hear," *Psychology Today*, August 1, 2012, https://www .psychologytoday.com/us/blog/words-can-change-your-brain/201208/why -word-is-so-dangerous-say-or-hear.

5. Therese J. Borchard, "Words Can Change Your Brain," Psych Central, January 2018, https://psychcentral.com/blog/words-can-change-your-brain-2.

6. Borchard, "Words Can Change Your Brain."

7. L. Manfra et al., "Preschoolers' Motor and Verbal Self-Control Strategies during a Resistant-to-Temptation Task," PubMed.gov, August 2014, https:// pubmed.ncbi.nlm.nih.gov/25175682/.

8. A. Latinjak et al., "Goal-Directed Self-Talk Used to Self-Regulate in Male Basketball Competitions," PubMed.gov, June 2019, https://pubmed.ncbi.nlm .nih.gov/30616448/.

9. P. Wallace et al., "Effects of Motivational Self-Talk on Endurance and Cognitive Performance in the Heat," PubMed.gov, January 2017, https://pubmed.ncbi.nlm.nih.gov/27580154/.

Chapter 5 LIE: "You are still a horrible sinner."

1. "Regeneration," *New Oxford American Dictionary* (New York: Oxford University Press, 2019).

2. This course is titled *Armor of God* and can be found at www.armorof godstudy.com.

3. "Consider," *Merriam-Webster*, 2021, https://www.merriam-webster .com/dictionary/consider.

Chapter 6 LIE: "God is punishing you."

1. Robert Jamieson et al., *A Commentary, Critical and Explanatory, on the Old and New Testaments*, 1 Jn 3:4 (Oak Harbor, Wash.: Logos Research Systems, 1997).

Chapter 8 LIE: "You cannot be forgiven."

1. "The Law," BibleProject, 2021, https://bibleproject.com/learn/the-law/.

Chapter 9 LIE: "You should be afraid."

1. Rebecca Stanborough, "Understanding and Overcoming Fear of the Unknown," Healthline, July 23, 2020, https://www.healthline.com/health /understanding-and-overcoming-fear-of-the-unknown.

2. Seth J. Gillihan, "How Often Do Your Worries Actually Come True?" *Psychology Today*, July 19, 2019, https://www.psychologytoday.com/us/blog /think-act-be/201907/how-often-do-your-worries-actually-come-true.

3. Josh Steimle, "14 Ways to Conquer Fear," Forbes, January 4, 2016, https://www.forbes.com/sites/joshsteimle/2016/01/04/14-ways-to-conquer -fear/?sh=190c73b91c48.

4. Walter Knight, "Don't Focus on Your Worries," Ministry 127, 2021, https://ministry127.com/resources/illustration/don-t-focus-on-your-worries.

Chapter 10 LIE: "You do not belong."

1. Neel Burton, "Our Hierarchy of Needs," *Psychology Today*, May 23, 2012, https://www.psychologytoday.com/us/blog/hide-and-seek/201205/our -hierarchy-needs.

2. Kelly Flanagan, *Loveable* (Grand Rapids: Zondervan, 2017), 138.

3. Dr. David DeWitt, "What Color Was Adam?" Answers in Genesis, February 20, 2021, https://answersingenesis.org/genetics/what-color-adam/.

4. "Quotes of Michaelangelo," Michaelangelo.org, 2012, https://www.michelangelo.org/michelangelo-quotes.jsp.

Chapter 11 LIE: "You need to be like somebody else."

1. Gigen Mammoser, "The FOMO Is Real: How Social Media Increases Depression and Loneliness," Healthline, December 9, 2018, https://www.healthline.com/health-news/social-media-use-increases-depression-and-loneliness.

2. Jacqueline Howard, "Americans Devote More Than 10 Hours a Day to Screen Time, and Growing," CNN, July 29, 2016, https://www.cnn.com/2016/06/30/health/americans-screen-time-nielsen/index.html.

3. Kristen Fuller, MD, "Social Media Breaks and Why They are Necessary," *Psychology Today*, July 1, 2019, https://www.psychologytoday.com/us/blog/happiness-is-state-mind/201907/social-media-breaks-and-why-they-are-necessary.

4. "Success," Webster's Dictionary 1828, February 24, 2020, http://webstersdictionary1828.com/Dictionary/success.

5. "Success," *Merriam-Webster*, 2021, https://www.merriam-webster.com/dictionary/success.

Chapter 12 LIE: "You have no purpose."

1. Anne Lamott, *Bird by Bird* (New York: Bantam Doubleday Dell, 1980), 236.

Chapter 13 LIE: "You are a failure."

1. NCC Staff, "Benjamin Franklin's Last Great Quote and the Constitution," Constitution Center, November 13, 2020, https://constitutioncenter.org/blog/benjamin-franklins-last-great-quote-and-the-constitution.

2. "Birthright," Bible Study Tools, 2021, https://www.biblestudytools.com/dictionary/birthright/.

3. "Blessing," Bible Study Tools, 2021, https://www.biblestudytools.com/dictionary/blessing/.

Chapter 14 LIE: "You are disqualified."

1. For more insight into this, I highly recommend Pastor Steven Furtick's book, *(Un)qualified: How God Uses Broken People to Do Big Things* (Colorado Springs: Multnomah, 2016).

2. Philip Cobb, "The 6 Biggest Drawbacks to Being an Extrovert," Inc.com, May 10, 2017, https://www.inc.com/quora/the-6-biggest-drawbacks-to-being-an-extrovert.html.

Kyle Winkler is a practical Bible teacher and creator of the popular Shut Up, Devil! mobile app. He is known for his vulnerable but bold messages that have been shared on platforms and media throughout the world, including TBN's *Praise the Lord*, Sid Roth's *It's Supernatural!*, *700 Club Interactive*, *The Blaze*, and many more. To get there, however, he first had to overcome deep wounds of rejection, shame and insecurity. With God's grace, he did. That is why he is so passionate about helping others find victory in their own struggles. Kyle holds a master of divinity in biblical studies from Regent University. He resides in central Florida.

To schedule Kyle to speak at your church or event, please email scheduling@kylewinkler.org.

Connect with Kyle:

kylewinkler.org

  @kylewinklerministries

  @kylewinklerministries

  @kylejwinkler

  @kylewinkler

More from Kyle Winkler

Shut Up, Devil! app

Put the power of God's Word in your pocket with personalized scriptures to declare over any issue you face. Available in your app store.

Experience Freedom album

65 minutes of spoken Scripture, backed by instrumental music, guide you into freedom and peace. Available on CD or iTunes.